Shortcuts to A Perfect Sewing Pattern

Written and Illustrated by
Rusty Bensussen

 Sterling Publishing Co., Inc.   New York

This book is dedicated to the wonderful people who make it all possible . . . most particularly

> *My editor, Barbara Busch, who gracefully puts everything into perspective . . . from introduction to epilogue.*
> *Karen Nelson, Art Director . . . for those beautiful covers.*

Library of Congress Cataloging-in-Publication Data

Bensussen, Rusty.
    Shortcuts to a perfect sewing pattern/written and illustrated by Rusty Bensussen.
        p.   cm.
    Includes index.
    ISBN 0-8069-6822-2 (pbk.)
    1. Dressmaking—Pattern design.   I. Title. II. Title: Sewing pattern.
TT520.B49 1989   88-30833
646.4'304—dc19   CIP

3 5 7 9 10 8 6 4 2

Copyright © 1989 by Estelle Bensussen
Published by Sterling Publishing Co., Inc.
Two Park Avenue, New York, N.Y. 10016
Distributed in Canada by Oak Tree Press Ltd.
c/o Canadian Manda Group, P.O. Box 920, Station U
Toronto, Ontario, Canada M8Z 5P9
Distributed in Great Britain and Europe by Cassell PLC
Artillery House, Artillery Row, London SW1P 1RT, England
Distributed in Australia by Capricorn Ltd.
P.O. Box 665, Lane Cove, NSW 2066
Manufactured in the United States of America

CONTENTS

Fig. 1. Repeating the same corrections on every pattern could
be a headache.

INTRODUCTION

Open the envelope of a commercial pattern and you might awaken a feeling of helplessness almost as severe as the response to the first pattern you ever held in your hands (Fig. 1).

When you were just beginning to sew, you had no idea of what to do with all those little pieces of tissue. Now that you know how to handle them, you're not sure that you really want to. You hope that each new pattern will fit properly as it comes from the envelope; experience tells you it most likely won't. Once again, you're facing pattern corrections that you really don't want to make.

Commercial patterns rarely fit the people who buy them because they are not made to order for any one individual (Fig. 2). They are produced for a mythical "Miss, Mrs. or Ms. Average Person," a creation of the National Bureau of Standards. This office conducts surveys across the United States and compiles personal measurements from thousands of people. The collected measurements are then averaged to find the proportions and range for each specific size group. Commercial pattern companies use these averages for the sizing of their patterns—the patterns you eventually buy.

Sounds O.K. so far, but here's the rub: When national size averages change drastically over a period of years, pattern companies are slow to adopt the new figures or change their slopers to meet current statistics. Their sizing sometimes lags as much as ten or more years behind national standards. This means that the measurements used by commercial pattern companies produce patterns that get farther and farther away from the actual requirements of the sewing public.

A few pattern companies have tried to meet the public needs by producing multisize patterns (Fig. 3). These were designed to remedy the many adjustments required by multisized figures. They were designed to compensate for individual body proportions and reduce the need for myriad pattern corrections. Each pattern includes a choice of three cutting lines for each segment, variations for figures with more than 10-inch differences between bust, waist and hips (the "ideal" dimensions).

Fig. 2. Commercial patterns come in mysterious sizes.

5

The concept was great; the result was not. The patterns did not accomplish the purpose for which they were designed. The idea of assorted widths for each pattern segment is an important advance, but pattern companies gave with one hand and took away with the other. They added length to the patterns with each width increase. This makes no sense: wider is not *always* taller; narrower is not *always* shorter.

In other words, all size 8's are not 5 feet tall, all size 18's are not 6 feet tall (Fig. 4). The result: You, the consumer, are just about where you started. Almost every pattern purchased still requires extensive personal adjustment before it is laid out on the fabric, and that still means a lot of work.

Although it's very tiresome, effort spent on fitting your patterns correctly is not wasted; it does pay dividends in the long run. You are striving for the perfect fit—one of the most important factors in the final appearance of a garment. The garments you enjoy most were cut from patterns that underwent some adjustment or personalizing (your

means of assuring the fit of each item when it was completed). That's why you can't resent completely the time invested in fitting a pattern. Just don't waste additional time by repeating the whole process of pattern corrections every time you prepare to sew. There is a shortcut you can take to achieve perfection. Create a *sloper* for each of the three basic garments: top, pants and skirt. With a personal sloper you will have the security of knowing that the garments you craft will fit to perfection every time (Fig. 5).

A personal sloper is a perfect-fit permanent pattern, which includes all of your required adjustments: a two-dimensional graphic form of your measurement chart. It is one of the most important sewing tools you can own. Using your sloper as a matrix or guide, corrections are easily traced onto commercial patterns without any remeasuring, new garments are cut without purchasing additional patterns, and new patterns can be created from your own fashion designs.

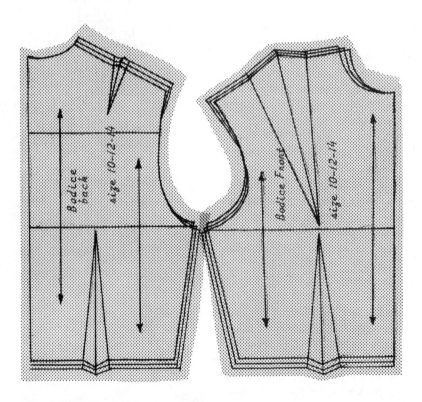

Fig. 3. Multisize patterns are available.

Fig. 4. Heavyset does not always mean tall; slender does not always mean short.

Fig. 5. Clothes that fit
properly get the most use.

If this sounds a little overwhelming, don't let it scare you. Simply translated, this means that whether you are a novice or an experienced seamstress, creating a perfect wardrobe is a sewing possibility.

An elegant wardrobe is the result of calculated choices, precisely taken measurements and applied technical knowledge. It is the end result of confidence in your fashion decisions, accommodation of your life style and careful coordination of new additions to existing clothing. An elegant wardrobe is made of skilfully crafted items from your own sewing machine combined with a personalized selection of ready-made clothing.

Absolute control over your fashion decisions is not a constitutional right; it is an acquired art. Confidence in your fashion decisions is the result of more than simple desire; you have to *do* something to fulfil that goal.

Before you rush to your closet to make space for all the perfect clothes you plan to sew, make a probing search of your fashion aims and desires. Look at your reflection in a full-length mirror and ask yourself some important questions about how you look and how you want to look—and give yourself some honest answers (Fig. 6).

The following questions might help put some of your fashion thoughts into perspective (Fig. 7).

1. What are your personal fashion aims? Have you determined a direction for your fashion choices? How do you really want to look? To dress? To present yourself? Do you give careful consideration to your life style before you sew or buy your clothing?

2. Have you done any personal color planning? What are your best personal color choices? What color range will flatter your hair? Your eyes? Your complexion?

3. What can you learn from a personal figure survey? Do you know which styles can maximize your best features and minimize any figure imbalance? Which style of clothing gives you the greatest versatility? The maximum service? Are you choosing the fabric best suited to the clothing you sew? To your figure?

4. Are you ready to take your personal body measurements? Are you ready to complete a personal measurement chart and work out your basic slopers?

Fig. 6. How do you really look?

9

Fig. 7. Coordinating your separates.

(This is necessary before you attempt to take your wardrobe in a new direction.) Do you take your personal measurements carefully and write them down as they actually are or do you hedge a little when you don't like the real numbers? Do you keep your measurement chart current?

Plot a sensible course for wardrobe changes. Determine how much time you can actually devote to yourself, and where you can best apply this valuable time. Include a rational budget allotment for sewing or buying new clothing and keep within your boundaries.

If you are serious about improving your image, this is the time to make decisions involving the way you look and the way you would prefer to look. It's never too late or too early to take command of your personal presentation to the world. Change can be rewarding at any time in your life. Knowing who you are and how you want to look is the first step towards achieving personal elegance and adding that desirable attitude of confidence. And please note: Elegance is not determined by the size printed on the label inside your clothing (Fig. 8). You can be elegant in a size 2, a size 22, a size 42, or any other number. A quality appearance is the total presentation of the individual, not the size of the clothing that covers the body.

Dressing well doesn't have to be a problem. With proper information, honest self-scrutiny and a little effort on your part, you can achieve any goals you seriously desire. You can learn more about your many choices, create the slopers to perfect the fit of your clothing, adorn your body with beautiful coverings, design the wardrobe you always wanted to wear, and have confidence in following your personal fashion instincts.

The following pages contain the information you need for making patterns fit the way they should. There is a simple and logical approach to choosing personal styles for your wardrobe and the details to get you started designing the patterns for all the beautiful clothing you've dreamed about.

As you go through the information, just keep one important thought in mind: *It's your body, and how you cover it is your choice.* Now, learn how to make these choices wisely.

Fig. 8. Elegance is not a size; it's a state of mind.

CHOOSING A SILHOUETTE

When you cover yourself merely for the sake of decency, you put on clothes with little or no thought of what you've assembled or how you look. You probably just pull a random assortment of clothing from your closet and toss it in the general direction of your body (Fig. 9). But when you really care about how you look and have a desire for personal identity, you begin to question the suitability of every item surveyed. When you care, getting dressed can be fraught with indecision and confusion.

Dressing well requires a careful, calculated, one-by-one selection of garments. Each piece of clothing is chosen from what already exists in your closet and is rated on the basis of how well it fits, how well it suits you, and how well it blends with the clothes already assembled. Your goal is to arrive at your own special look and a workable costume (Fig. 10). You strive for the ultimate in chic. Somewhere along the line you might be willing to settle for a touch of something near elegance, but too often what results from these private debates is a headache and feeling of insecurity from not actually *knowing* what to wear or how to wear it.

While trying to translate a dim mental image into a finished costume, you often have a feeling of total helplessness. Following half-formed fashion instincts is difficult. Harboring a secret mental image that is the same as reality is very fulfilling; however, most private aspirations are far beyond the results actually achieved. Does your general appearance lean towards being well-groomed and elegantly dressed, or are you just sort of thrown together? Take a serious look at your reflection, add up your assets and isolate figure defects. Judge your reflection objectively to determine where your general appearance could use a little help.

The lines of the clothing you choose have a definite effect on your total appearance. Information on basic style-lines can be a useful directory through a maze of fashion decisions. Knowing which silhouette makes you look taller or shorter, slender or more curvaceous, puts you in the position of creating the effect you've always desired.

Fig. 9. Getting dressed shouldn't be a game of blindman's buff.

12

There are three basic silhouettes to consider; one category can strengthen your fashion image. Each style will disguise a different figure problem; each can enhance different assets. The basic silhouettes are: the A-line, the V-line and the straight-line.

Fig. 10. A very workable costume.

The A-Line

The A-line or inverted wedge is the most complimentary style for the bottom-heavy figure (Fig. 11). It is narrow at the top to fit the shoulders, then flares to the lower edge, allowing ample room for easy, natural movement. The A-line provides graceful coverage for heavy hips and thighs without undue definition of the lower body. The general shape of the A-line draws the eye towards the upper portion of the body, calling attention to the head, neck and shoulders, emphasizing the more slender areas. It is an ideal line to choose if you are trying to minimize extra girth below the waist.

Fig. 11. The A-line.

The V-Line

The V-line or true wedge puts the major portion of the fabric at the top, towards the shoulder line. This provides ample coverage for an abundant bust and shoulder line, minimizing the upper portion of the body in the lines of the design (Fig. 12).

The V-line is a good style for the top-heavy figure, as it narrows towards the hips, accenting the slimness of the lower portion of the body. Since the direction of the V-line points down, it draws attention to slender proportions of the hips and nicely shaped legs.

Fig. 12. The V-line.

The Straight-Line

The straight-line garment is the style to choose when your proportions are fairly equal (Fig. 13). Whether you are slim as the proverbial reed or on the heavy side, a straight-line garment is flattering. "Straight" means that the coverage of the garment is equal throughout, the fabric evenly distributed between the top and bottom with no wide flares, gores, or excessive gathers. What straight does *not* mean is tight. An easy fit in this or any style is always more flattering to the figure than a skimpy, sausage-casing look. An even flow of fabric has its own elegance.

At some point in life, each woman becomes aware of her own figure and strives to emphasize her best features. She wants to dress well, in comfortable clothing, bearing her own personal identity. Where most fail to achieve a satisfactory wardrobe is in a lack of style consistency. One day you're dressed like a model; the next day you're dressed like any stranger you might pass on the street. This random style of dressing does not necessarily suit your figure, build or coloring. It isn't the perfection you're after.

The first order of elegance is to choose a flattering line or silhouette and stick with it—a style suited to your particular figure, a general shape or "look" for each item or an entire costume.

Choosing a personal silhouette does not lock you in to a uniform, a single style, a boring sameness throughout your entire wardrobe for the rest of your life. There are a lot of variations possible within each given fashion, and they are created with style-ease.

Fig. 13. The straight-line.

16

Definition: Style-Ease

Style-ease is the addition or subtraction of fabric to *modify* a basic design or give a totally new and different look to a familiar pattern. It is a way of extending a design or devising completely new and exciting creations without losing the basic concept of a particular style (Fig. 14).

It really isn't difficult to extend a chosen fashion; you can revamp the fit of any garment. There are even terms to define these style variations. You've probably seen these words on commercial pattern envelopes without paying any attention to them, but they describe the type or amount of style-ease in each design and explain some of the potential variations for basic styles.

Fig. 14. Reshape a familiar pattern with style-ease.

Fitted: Garments in this category closely follow the contours of the body (Fig. 15). The lines define each curve and bone. A well-proportioned, slender body is enhanced by a fitted style.

Semi-Fitted: This type of design fits smoothly over the bust and lightly skims the waist and hips (Fig. 16). It shows off a nicely formed upper body without emphasizing a less-than-perfect lower body.

Slightly Fitted: Although this style follows the general shape of the body, it does so loosely.

Slightly-fitted fashions display considerable style-ease throughout the entire garment, providing room to flow softly over your contours (Fig. 17).

Loosely Fitted: The fullness of these garments starts above the bustline and falls loosely to the hem (Fig. 18). They include the deep dolman or raglan sleeve, oversized top and luxuriously full pants and skirts.

You can readjust a pattern to suit your figure or chosen silhouette by making adjustments to the amount of style-ease already included in the pat-

Fig. 15. Fitted styles

Fig. 16. Semi-fitted lines

Fig. 17. Slightly-fitted clothes

Fig. 18. Loosely-fitted styles

tern design. Personal adjustments are the secret of making commercial patterns work like personal designs.

Do not take style-ease into consideration when choosing a pattern size. Choosing a pattern in a smaller size because the design looks roomy will only negate the stylish lines of the finished garment and probably destroy the fit.

A typical example of an augmented style is the "Big Shirt" (Fig. 19). It is an extension of a simple, man-tailored shirt style. The patterns for a big shirt may look as though they could fit two people at the same time, but don't be fooled. Most patterns for oversized garments have some point at which they closely fit the body. For example, the fit might come at the armhole and extend over part of the sleeve, and a size 18 arm will never fit comfortably into a size 8 armhole and sleeve, even if the rest of the pattern appears to fit properly.

Wear-Ease

Wear-ease, on the other hand, is the ease built into the pattern to allow for freedom of movement, the added dimension beyond your actual body measurements. Wear-ease provides the room within each garment to sit or stand comfortably, to walk with grace and reach without straining seams and fabric beyond endurance.

Wear-ease creates the space to bend your knees, elbows or entire body, without creating permanent knee, seat and elbow sag in your clothing (Fig. 20). It is the difference between fabric being wrapped so tightly around your body that it looks painted on and fabric hanging gracefully from shoulder to hemline.

In other words, wear-ease is the added dimension that gives woven garments the comfort of knits. It is built into all patterns in varying amounts—from infant sizes through queen sizes. Wear-ease is the reason you so carefully take personal measurements. These are the inches beyond your actual dimensions that you will add when you design a pattern or achieve a personal fit.

There are exceptions to every rule and the rules governing ease-allowance change when dealing with knits: Wear-ease is built into all unbonded,

Fig. 19. The "Big Shirt" is an extension of a more fitted style.

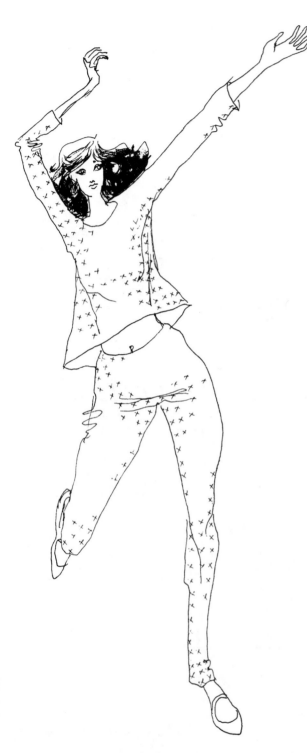

knitted fabric. This is the reason that pattern envelopes indicate suitable fabrics for each garment. Patterns designed for *knitted fabrics only* do not include additional wear-ease; the yardage must have natural give. It can be converted for use with woven fabrics *IF* you carefully compare the pattern measurements to your own and add the proper amounts of wear-ease to the design.

The following charts define the amount of wear-ease required to build comfort into the patterns you design. Your figure-type will tell you which chart category is best suited to your use.

Standard Wear-Ease: Juniors and Misses

Bust	2″ to 3″
Waist	¾″
Hip	1¾″ to 2½″
Crotch	½″ to ¾″

Standard Wear-Ease: Women's Sizes

Bust	3½″ to 4½″
Waist	½″ to ¾″ (dress)
Hip	2½″ to 2¾″ (skirt)

Don't confuse wear-ease with style-ease when you read the information charts on a pattern and don't short one for the other. Wear-ease (comfort ease) and style-ease (reshaping for a new or extended design) are both in addition to your actual measurements. When buying a commercial pattern, you don't have to add these allowances to your actual measurements: The pattern maker has included style-ease in creating the design and wear-ease in the shaping of the pattern. When drafting a pattern of your own, wear-ease must be added. When designing your own fashions, the style-ease is in the design you create.

Using Style-Ease to Extend a Design

Once you have chosen the most flattering general silhouette for your wardrobe, use style-ease to create new fashions. These styles: A-line, V-line and straight-line are easily varied. Each has a way of drawing the eye-of-the-beholder towards your best features or special assets; extending the design will not change the basic lines.

Fig. 20. Wear-ease shapes the fabric to cover the body comfortably.

- The basic A-line shape drifts gently from the shoulder to the hemline. It can also sweep from shoulders to waist, waist to hem, giving a tiered effect.

- It is still an A-line even if it is somewhat fitted to the waistline and flares to the hemline; the choice is yours (Fig. 21). Any way you wear it, the A-line fashion is flattering to the A-line figure.

Fig. 21. Extending the A-line.

• The lines of the V-shaped dress can drape generously at the top and gather into a snugly sashed hipline (Fig. 22).

• If may also start from a lightly padded shoulder and taper to the hem (Fig. 23). Both sketches demonstrate ways to minimize broad shoulders or a large bosom.

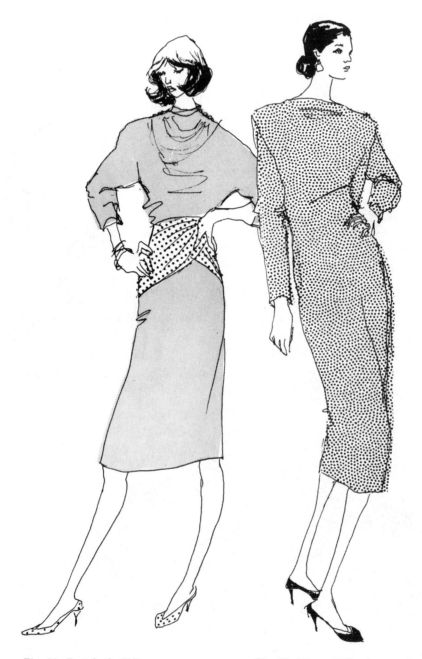

Fig. 22. Restyle the V-line.　　　　*Fig. 23. Wear a V-line loose and easy.*

- The straight silhouette may literally fall straight from the shoulders to the hem.

- Wear a straight-line dress belted at the rib cage, waist or hip (Fig. 24).

- A straight-line garment can have a knife-pleated front and/or back, one side or both. Again, the choice is yours.

Fig. 24. Place a belt anywhere you like.

About Hemlines

The lengths you choose for the garments you make determine the final appearance of those garments; hemlines do influence the look of the silhouette. Choosing a personal hemline is probably one of the single most difficult fashion decisions a woman has to make. Even when you think you know how long you want your skirt, there are outside influences that force some changes. When the majority of the female population is wearing very short skirts (the mini, for example), you can feel as if you're in a nightgown if you wear your skirts at mid-calf. When most women wear their skirts at mid-calf length, you feel and look half-undressed if still wearing micro-minis. That's the public side of hemlines.

The private side of hemlines is that the lengths of your skirts and dresses have a decided effect on your silhouette.

A longer skirt adds height to your general appearance if you are of average height or above, but an ankle-length or mid-calf skirt can swallow a short woman (Fig. 25).

A short skirt (above the knee) will certainly display a shapely pair of legs, but if you have a stocky torso a short skirt makes it appear even broader (Fig. 26). In the same vein, a full skirt (wide A-line or a very full-gathered dirndl) will appear longer than a slim, straight-line skirt of the same length.

Your height, weight, age, general build and the shapeliness of your legs should be all taken into consideration when making hemline choices. The weight of the fabric chosen for a particular garment can also result in changes to the positioning of your hemline. There is a rule of thumb for finding a starting point for your hem length: 2″ below the knee will put the hem at a flattering position for *most* legs. So where do *you* place a hemline? You place it, with confidence and conviction, in the best *personal* location; the length of skirt *you* need to feel comfortable and well dressed. You always have the final word when making personal choices.

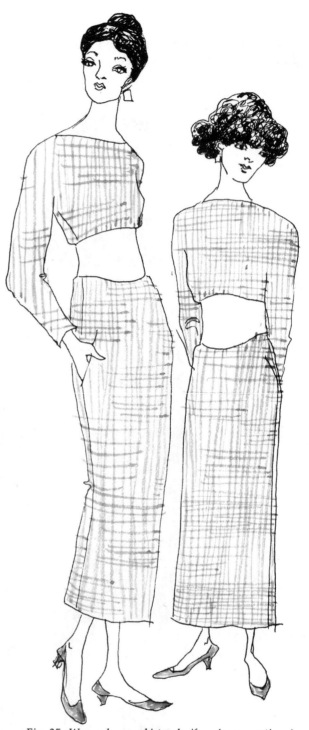

Fig. 25. *Wear a longer skirt only if you're proportioned for it.*

Fig. 26. *Short skirts can display more than you intend to show.*

chosen for that style but allow a little extra at the hemline for adjustments before hemming.

Footnotes to Personal Fashion

When choosing ready-made clothing or patterns and fabric for your sewing, don't go off on tangents because of the way others are dressed. What you need to know is that the style, shape and fabric is right for *you!*

Be consistent in your personal style. Consistency is a confidence builder. There is no way you can look and feel your best when each outfit in your wardrobe presents a totally different personal picture—and not always a flattering picture. You never want to look as if you were thrown together by committee.

Fig. 27. *Try a variety of hemlines.*

Placing Your Hemline

There is no substitute for seeing how you look in a variety of hem placements. Take a length of fabric to your mirror, drape the material around your body and adjust it to various positions along your leg (Fig. 27). Each time you arrive at a location that pleases you, measure the length of the fabric from the waistline to the bottom edge. Take note of each length that you might find usable.

Push more of the fabric to the front of your body to see the effect of a full skirt at different lengths. Keep readjusting the fabric until you have several usable answers that satisfy you both in appearance and comfort and write those figures on your chart. When you cut a garment, use the length you've

A Very Personal Assessment

Fit is carefully measured into the pattern, not forced into the finished garment.

Achieving a perfect fit is the goal of every woman who uses a sewing machine. After all, who doesn't yearn for a beautiful wardrobe? But beautiful clothing doesn't just happen; it is the reward for invested effort.

You start with a critical analysis of your figure, collect a series of accurate personal measurements, then enter these honest numbers on your measurement chart for current and future use. This personal measurement chart that you carefully complete is a numeric description of your figure—every curve, muscle and indentation.

The next step is to transpose the chart into a sloper, a perfect-fit permanent pattern (Fig. 28). Your sloper is the basic pattern that you use as a matrix or map to correct commercial patterns to suit your figure, cut basic clothing without any additional patterns or create patterns from your own designs.

Measurements for your chart *cannot* be adjusted or faked; "close" or "almost" isn't good enough. The numbers are written exactly as they read; they reflect your body. Correct measurements guarantee sewing results you may never have experienced before.

Clothing only fits to perfection when you start with perfect measurements. You'll have a new feeling of physical comfort from the garments you craft, and the security of knowing that everything you sew will hang properly and look the way you intended. When you are well dressed you will like yourself better than before. The reality: You *can* look the way you always dreamed you could.

The nice part about taking your own measurements is that the information you get from your tape measure is private. You won't have to share it with anyone, so you won't be tempted to fudge the numbers. They'll be usable because they are accurate.

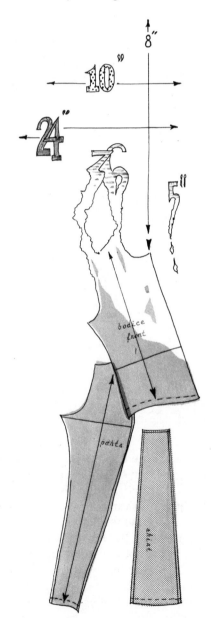

Fig. 28. Personal measurements are the key to your sloper.

What to Wear for a Figure Assessment

Take your measurements in the type of under-clothing you customarily wear or, at most, put on a leotard (Fig. 29). Neither will change the true dimensions or proportions of your body. Forget the waist cinch, tight girdle to minimize your hips or padded bra to accent your bosom if you only wear these figure-enhancers on rare occasions.

Personal Measurement Chart: General Information

Take all measurements with an accurate tape measure. A plastic-coated fabric tape will do, but avoid plain, uncoated fabric tapes as they stretch, giving inconsistent measurements.

You need a pen or pencil and copies of each of the measurement charts from this book. You can write your computations directly into the book, but a photocopy or tracing of the charts is more practical and portable. The original charts will remain for future use.

Record each measurement in the appropriate space; the numbers won't be misunderstood or lost when they are labelled properly. Fill in all the blanks on your personal chart in consecutive order. Follow each direction and/or illustration. Start from the top and work down to be sure you have completed all the necessary information.

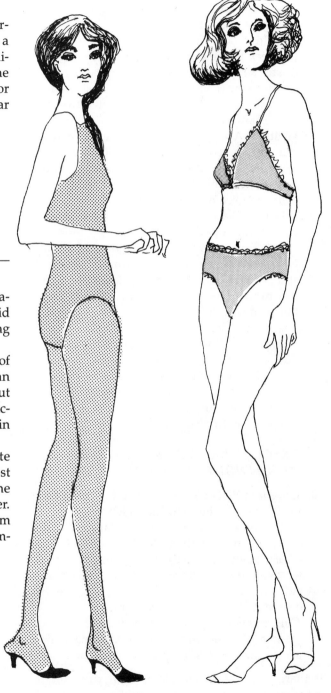

Fig. 29. Simple body coverings won't interfere with correct measurements.

PERSONAL MEASUREMENT CHART #1:
FRONT WIDTHS (Fig. 30).

1. **Neck:** Wrap the tape measure comfortably around the base of your neck for your collar size. Don't pull the tape too tight or your collars will never fit.
2. **Shoulder Length:** Measure from the base of the neck to the outer point of the shoulder.
3. **Bust:** Wrap the tape measure completely around your chest: across the widest point of the back, under the arms, and across the apex of the bosom.
4. **Width of Apex:** Measure the distance between the nipples across the apex of the bosom.
5. **Front Across Bosom:** Note the measurement across the front of the body, over the bosom, from side seam to side seam.
6. **Ribcage:** Place the tape completely around your chest below the bustline.
7. **Waist:** Tie a string or lightweight cord around your waistline and measure around your waist at this line. Leave the cord in place after taking this measurement as it will be used for additional measurements.
8. **High Hip:** Measure around the fullest part of the hipline, 7″ to 9″ below your natural waistline.
9. **Low Hip:** Measure around the low point of your hipline approximately 12″ below the natural waistline, around the buttocks and high point of the thighs.

PERSONAL MEASUREMENT CHART #2:
FRONT LENGTH MEASUREMENTS (Fig. 31).

10. **Length to Waist:** Measure from the base of the neck, over the bust, to the waistline.
11. **Collarbone to Waist:** Drop the tape from the center of the collarbone to the waistline. This measurement is particularly important to women who do not wear a B-cup bra as it provides an accurate measurement of the length differential for your bodice front.
12. **Collarbone to Apex:** From the base of the neck (center of collarbone) to an imaginary line across the nipples or apex of the bosom.

If there is no one available to scan your length measurements, you can handle them by yourself. Attach a small weight to the bottom of your tape measure. Hold the middle of the tape between

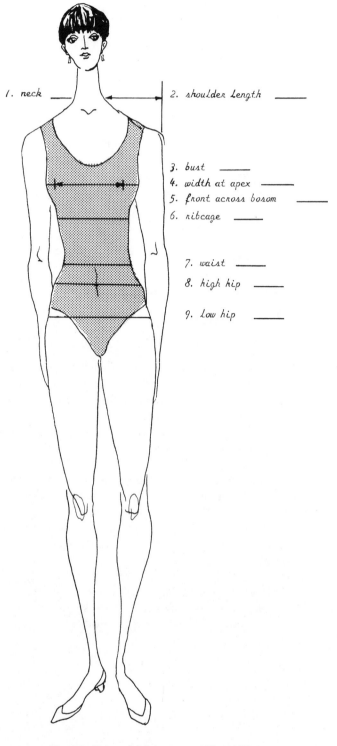

Fig. 30. Personal Measurement Chart #1: Front (Widths)

your index finger and thumb, allowing approximately 30 inches to dangle. Stand in front of a full-length mirror and place your fingers (holding the tape) at the base of your neck (for a full-length

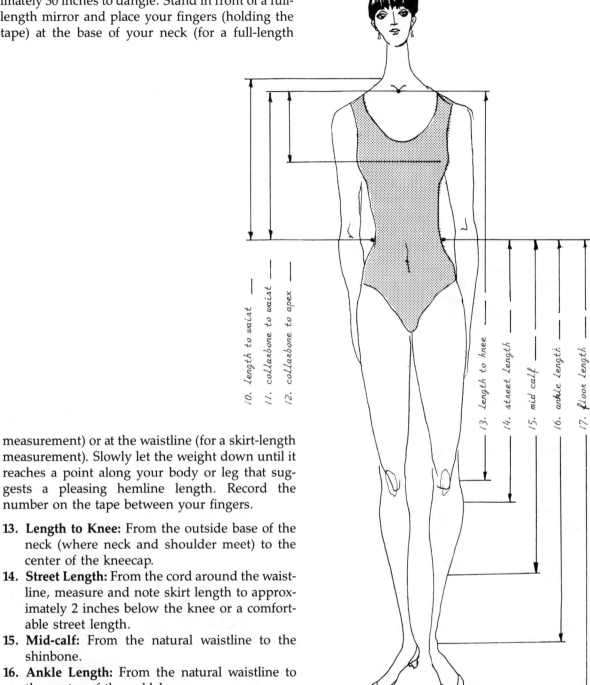

measurement) or at the waistline (for a skirt-length measurement). Slowly let the weight down until it reaches a point along your body or leg that suggests a pleasing hemline length. Record the number on the tape between your fingers.

13. **Length to Knee:** From the outside base of the neck (where neck and shoulder meet) to the center of the kneecap.
14. **Street Length:** From the cord around the waistline, measure and note skirt length to approximately 2 inches below the knee or a comfortable street length.
15. **Mid-calf:** From the natural waistline to the shinbone.
16. **Ankle Length:** From the natural waistline to the center of the anklebone.
17. **Floor Length:** Measure from the natural waistline to the floor. (Add any other lengths you might use.)

Fig. 31. Personal Measurement Chart #2: Front (Lengths)

PERSONAL MEASUREMENT CHART #3:
SLEEVES (Fig. 32).

18. **Sleeve Length:** With hand on hip, arm slightly flexed, measure from the shoulder joint to the wristbone.
19. **Shoulder to Elbow:** Record the length from shoulder joint to the center of the elbow for sleeve-dart placement.
20. **Upper Arm:** Flex your arm and measure around the bicep for upper-sleeve fit.
21. **Elbow:** Measure and record the circumference of the elbow.
22. **Wrist:** Measure circumference of the wrist.

PERSONAL MEASUREMENT CHART #4:
UPPER BACK (Fig. 33).

Simplify your alterations by having very detailed measurements on the chart rather than taking separate measurements each time you sew. Carefully note the back measurements from side seam to side seam. Don't just divide a total body measurement in half for your back measurements; measure each portion of your body. Back and front dimensions are not necessarily equal.

23. **High Back:** Jot down the back measurement from side seam to side seam along bra line.
24. **Rib Cage:** Back portion of the measurement, side seam to side seam, below bustline.
25. **Waistline:** The measurement across the back of the natural waistline, from side seam to side seam.
26. **High Hip:** Across the fullest part of the hipline, to 9 inches below your natural waistline.
27. **Low Hip:** Across the low point of the hipline, approximately 12 inches below the natural waistline.

PERSONAL MEASUREMENT CHART #5:
BACK LENGTH (Fig. 34).

28. **Length to Waist:** Measure from the last bone at the base of the neck (back) to the natural waistline where the string is tied.
29. **Dress Length:** Measure from the base of the neck to approximately 2 inches below the knee or your comfortable hem length.
30. **Skirt Length:** Note your back length from waistline to hem of chosen length. If you are

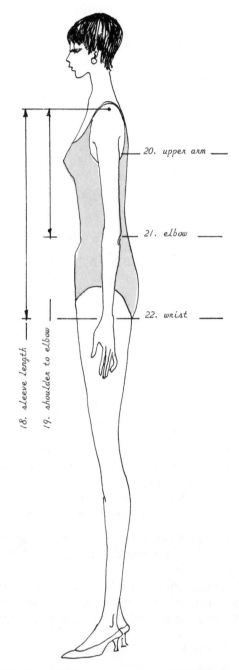

Fig. 32. Personal Measurement Chart #3: Sleeves

somewhat swaybacked, this is an important measurement as front and back lengths will not be the same.

31. **Mid-calf:** Record length to mid-shinbone.

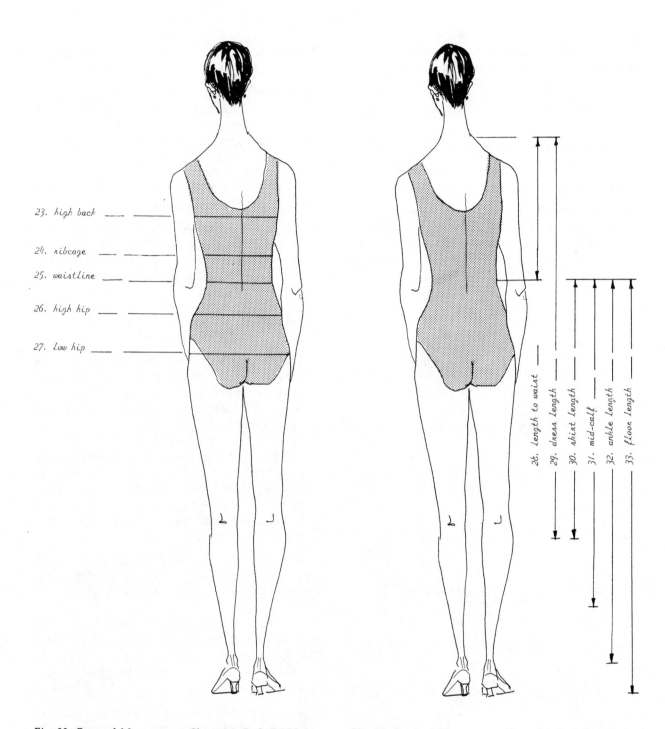

23. high back ____

24. ribcage ____

25. waistline ____

26. high hip ____

27. low hip ____

28. length to waist ____
29. dress length ____
30. skirt length ____
31. mid-calf ____
32. ankle length ____
33. floor length ____

Fig. 33. Personal Measurement Chart #4: Back (Widths)   *Fig. 34. Personal Measurement Chart #5: Back (Lengths)*

32. Ankle Length: Drop the tape from the natural waistline to the middle of the ankle.

33. Floor Length: Note the length from the waist to the floor.

The following measurements can be noted along the edge of your chart. They are measurements that will ease your general sewing.

- The measurement from the shoulder to the low hip is a good length to keep a blouse properly tucked into the waistband of your skirt or pants.

- For overblouses and jackets, use the length from your shoulder to a point just below the buttocks.

- If you sew for sport activities, take any additional measurements you might use for specific clothing. Label each measurement with the appropriate activity: tennis skirt, golf skirt, ice-skating skirt, etc.

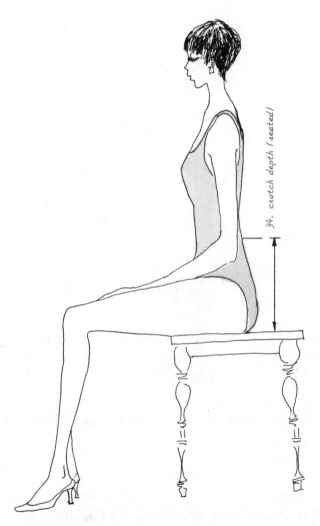

34. crotch depth (seated)

Fig. 35. Personal Measurement Chart #6: Pants (Seated)

PERSONAL MEASUREMENT CHART #6: *PANTS (SEATED) (Fig. 35)*

Making pants that fit properly is a feat that eludes many people. Use particular care in taking the following measurements; pant lines are *critical*. There is no way to disguise a poor fit; so recheck all measurements you take.

These measurements are in addition to the ones already taken. The cord tied around your waist will provide a consistent waistline location.

34. **Crotch Depth (SEATED):** Sit squarely on a firm chair or the coffee table with both feet planted on the floor. Measure the distance from your natural waistline to the tabletop.

PERSONAL MEASUREMENT CHART #7: *PANT LENGTH (Fig. 36)*

35. **Crotch Length (STANDING):** Attach the tape measure to the center back of the waistline cord, pull it between your legs and bring it up to meet the waistline at the front. Note the total measurement.

36. **In-seam:** Tie approximately 18″ of cord to a small weight and make a loop at the opposite end. Hang this loop from the tape, allowing the weight to slide to the center point of the body. This is your inseam location, an exact measurement for the length of the crotch curve, both front and back.

The crotch line is a very important measurement. It is the point-of-fit for any pair of pants. This measurement is worth double-checking.

- If you have a large posterior or a protruding tummy, the crotch-line measurement provides the space, both front and back, to accommodate the body properly and retain the fit of the finished pants.

- The waistband will remain in the proper position while you are sitting or standing if the crotch line has the proper length.

- An adequate crotch line will allow the in-seam to center on the body; pants will hang straight from top to bottom. The inseam forms a straight line through the center of the body pointing to the base of the ear at the top, to the center of the anklebone at the bottom.

37. **Finished Length:** Drop a tape from the true waistline to the bottom of your anklebone for your pant-hem length.

38. **Length to Floor:** Take one additional length measurement: from the waistline to the floor. This measurement is usually equal to your length (when wearing flat-heeled shoes) plus the hem allowance. It's a handy figure to record for those times when you want to hem a pair of pants and no one is available to check the pinned length.

Personal Measurement Charts: Storage and Use

Keep your completed charts in plastic sleeves, prepunched to fit a ring binder. This will protect the pages from smears or smudges and reinforce your charts for long-term use. Store them carefully in your sewing notebook so that you'll always know where they are when needed.

When you go pattern shopping, take your charts with you. Compare your personal measurements with the measurements printed on the back of the pattern envelope. It is your assurance that you have chosen the pattern closest to your needs, the pattern that will require the least number of adjustments for a personalized fit. Don't worry about the size printed on the pattern; the important numbers are the measurements in inches, not the size category.

KEEP YOUR CHART CURRENT

Recheck the measurements on your chart every few months under normal conditions. Figures do change and physical changes are not as apparent to the eye as they are to the tape measure. If you are sewing while actively dieting, recheck your prime measurements each time you sew. The fit of a pattern can completely change with each 10 pounds your weight fluctuates.

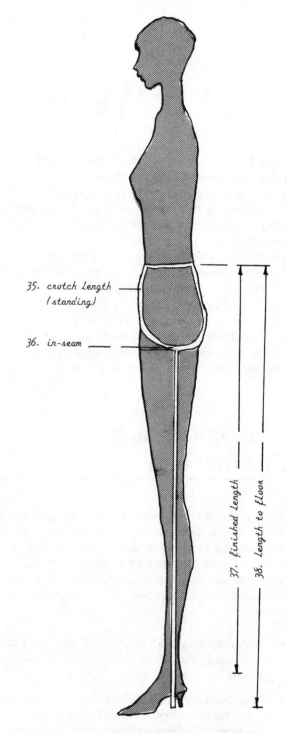

Fig. 36. Personal Measurement Chart #7: Pants (Length)

WHY A SLOPER?

Patterns are easy to adjust for personal fit *if* you have no major figure problems. Correcting the length of a sleeve, repositioning a hem, rounding or narrowing the hipline of a skirt or a pair of pants, adding or subtracting an inch or so at the waistline, can all be done without making any physical changes to the pattern (Fig. 37). Each of these minor adjustments can be handled along the outside edges of the pattern pieces during the cutting of the garment. But when a few simple cutting adjustments no longer solve your problems and the possibility of ever achieving a pattern fit seems remote, it's time to stop guessing about personal alterations and start making a sloper.

The Sloper as a Sewing Tool

Your personally adjusted permanent pattern or sloper is as important to the clothing you make as your sewing machine, scissors, pins or fabric. It is your image in the form of a flat pattern, the tool you will use to personalize commercial patterns and draft new patterns from your own designs. For example:

- Slopers can be placed underneath any tissue pattern to verify dimensions and correct commercial patterns for personal use.

- Crotch lines are critical points on a pants pattern. With a current sloper you can trace all personal adjustments (including the crotch line) onto a commercial pattern to make the general design of the pattern fit your figure.

- Correct a pant pattern that was used once and filed away because of a poor fit. Trace the personal fitting lines of your sloper to the tissue pattern. Tape extra pieces of tissue paper to the commercial pattern in any areas that need enlarging. Grade pattern lines wherever corrections are made; any pattern can work for you.

- Use your sloper to trace length and width adjustments for hemlines, darts or seams onto any pattern. You won't have to do any additional measuring.

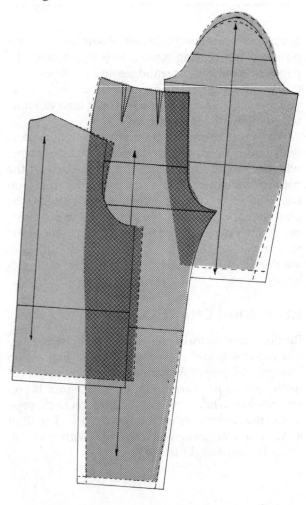

Fig. 37. Make minor adjustments along the seam lines of the pattern.

- Combine your bodice and skirt slopers to alter dress patterns to your measurements or create new dress patterns from your own designs (Fig. 38).

- Combine the bodice and pant slopers to adjust a commercial jumpsuit pattern or create patterns from your own designs (Fig. 39).

- Change the shape of an armhole on a bodice pattern (Fig. 40).

- Redesign a sleeve to update an old pattern.

Fig. 39. Jumpsuits can fit comfortably.

Fig. 38. Create new designs from your sloper.

The thought of drafting your own patterns may seem farfetched at this point, but, in reality, your sloper is a basic pattern waiting for your personal touches. You can draft patterns of your own design as easily as you can alter a commercial pattern. That measurement chart you labored over so carefully contains all the information you need; it is the guideline to creating your slopers.

Creating a Sloper: General Information

You don't even have to draft the patterns from your measurement chart to create your slopers; use commercial patterns for the general outlines and shaping. The tissue patterns can be cut and taped, adding or subtracting length or width wherever necessary to conform with your body measurements. If you feel that it might be easier to adjust a cloth pattern, trace the lines from the tissue onto inexpensive fabric or nonwoven pattern-drafting cloth, creating a working muslin.

An old sloper from a bygone era, which no longer fits properly (or possibly never did fit right), should be checked to see whether it can be corrected to your current measurements. Take it out, dust it off and press it (if it was folded for storage). It might be easier to update it than to adjust a complete commercial pattern. If the old sloper is too far away from your current measurements to be of value, try your own pattern file before shopping for new patterns to turn into slopers. You probably have patterns sitting in a drawer or box that will work very well: a tailored shirt pattern for the bodice sloper, a clean-line separate skirt and a simple pant pattern.

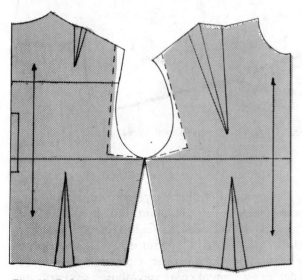

Fig. 40. Redesign the armhole opening.

Start from individual patterns rather than using the two halves of a dress or jumpsuit pattern. Pattern pieces that are designed to fit together don't always work well as separate units. Darts and side seams are jockeyed to meet, top and bottom, rather than positioned to enhance the separate parts.

If you must buy new patterns for conversion to slopers, use your completed measurement chart to help you select the correct size. Compare the measurements of your shoulders, bustline, waistline, high hips and low hips with those listed on the pattern envelope. The pattern with measurements closest to your own is the one to buy. If you fall between two size categories of commercial pant or skirt patterns, fit your hipline for the fewest pattern adjustments; the waistline can be altered more easily than the entire garment.

For the least adjustments on a bodice pattern, choose the pattern nearest your bustline measurements. (For additional information see "Drafting a Bodice Sloper," page 38.)

Before you begin drawing your sloper, recheck your measurement chart to be sure that all blanks have been filled in and all measurements have been taken according to the instructions. You will be using all the numbers that you so carefully assembled.

- Have a red, green or purple pen handy to draw highly visible, personal corrections on the original commercial pattern tissue.

- Trace the commercial pattern onto muslin or pattern drafting cloth with a blue pen. Use a contrasting color for the personal corrections.

- Draw final cutting lines with a wide-point black pen grading all new lines to meet the existing pattern lines. The assorted pen colors will simplify identification of all the lines on the pattern: Original printed lines, personal corrections and the final cutting lines you draw to your measurements.

Getting Started

If you use a tissue-paper pattern, unfold the segments and carefully press out all creases with a barely warm iron. It is very important that each major pattern piece be completely smooth before you begin, as creases and folds react like unplanned pleats: If they are not ironed out before cutting the garment, each segment could come out a different size.

Pin the prime segments of the pattern to the cutting board for personal sizing. Facings, interfacings, pockets and other accompaniments can be laid aside; a sloper deals only with the main pattern pieces.

Finishing Your Sloper

When all adjustments are indicated on the pattern or muslin, verify the corrections and complete all cutting lines. Check to be sure that new lines are graded to flow smoothly into the original pattern lines. Make sure that all darts are indicated and completed, fold lines and stitching lines redrawn wherever necessary. Double-check any variation you list: additional hemlines, sleeve lengths and styles, bodice variations. Make sure that everything you indicate is properly labelled. Check cutting notches and other construction information before transferring them to your sloper.

Transfer your personal pattern lines and all pertinent information to a permanent form by one of the following methods:

1. Bond the corrected, personalized pattern segments to heavy, nonwoven interfacing; or
2. Trace all lines and notations from the fitted pattern to a sheet of tagboard or other lightweight cardboard. Ink all lines, etc., and reinforce the pattern by covering with gummed, transparent film.

Prevent damage from unexpected moisture by using permanent ink to complete the drawings. Lines drawn in permanent ink cannot be washed away.

Choose any finishing form for your sloper that you prefer—as long as the finished pattern is sturdy enough to last through repeated use. A personally fitted sloper is a very precious item and should be finalized in a form that will survive repeated use over a long period of time.

Certainly, your first aim in creating these slopers is to perfect the fit of the garments you wear. The next in importance is to broaden the scope of your wardrobe and provide more variety in the clothing you wear (Fig. 41). You can create any number of new garments directly from your slopers; using a variety of fabrics will make the same pattern look new each time it is used.

With a good-fitting basic pattern, changing the design is not as important as changing the fabric.

Fig. 41. Enjoy variety and good fit.

DRAFTING A BODICE SLOPER

Drafting a bodice sloper is a much easier process when you start from a commercial pattern. Choose an uncomplicated, basic shirt style with set-in sleeves, merge the pattern with the information from your personal measurement chart, put the results into permanent form, and you have a perfect-fit sloper, a flat pattern that you can use with absolute confidence.

Choosing Your Pattern Size

Choose your pattern wisely. Balance the upper-body measurements in your personal chart against the information on the pattern envelope. Select the pattern with the greatest number of measurements that match your own. The size printed on the pattern envelope is not important; measurements give you the results you want (Fig. 42.)

Pattern alterations can be grouped into a few categories:

1. Universal adjustments such as the length of skirts, pants and sleeves;

2. Personal alterations made to accommodate individual figure proportions; and

3. Adjustments caused by choosing the wrong size pattern.

There is no definitive answer to hem placement; it even varies from garment to garment in your own closet. But hem placement does not affect the size of the patterns you choose; personal figure proportions do. If you have been making extensive adjustments on every pattern you buy, rethinking your pattern size might ease your problem and minimize the number of corrections you actually have to make. Your personal measurements will indicate which size pattern will serve you best: your usual size, a smaller pattern or a larger one.

Fig. 42. Use your sloper for beautiful results.

There is some quick-help information that can ease you through your pattern-size decisions.

• *General Fit:* When the shoulder line, darts and waistline are in the proper position but the general fit of the pattern feels too snug for easy movement, don't change your pattern for a larger size. This will throw off all the points where the pattern already fits your body. Do add to the width of the pattern without altering the shape of the design (Fig. 43).

Fig. 44. *Commercial patterns are scaled to a B-cup bra size.*

• *Bustline Fitting* is probably the most common headache of all the pattern adjustments. Commercial patterns are drafted to fit a B-cup bra size (Fig. 44). This obviously does not include all the women in the world. If you are part of that large segment of womanhood whose measurements do not fall into the B-cup-bra category, be sure you accommodate your total bustline measurement, your cup size, and your shoulder measurements when choosing your pattern. These are prime points-of-fit for a blouse or dress pattern, the final word on the fit of the pattern. Each of these garments hangs from the shoulder line.

If your bustline measurement is slightly larger than that of the pattern measurement but your cup size is a B, buy the same size pattern you would normally buy. The indication is that your back measurement is broader than the front of your body (Fig. 45). The alterations involve some simple adjustments to the back-pattern segment, not a size change.

Fig. 43. *Add width to the pattern without changing the basic lines.*

If your bra cup is a C or larger, you might need a larger-size pattern to properly locate the bust-line darts and/or fit chest and shoulder measurements (Fig. 46). It is often easier to adjust a few side seams on a larger-size pattern to accommodate a C-cup (or larger) size than it is to move darts and enlarge an entire blouse pattern that might never fit properly. Darts will be a little lower on the larger-size pattern and the armhole will probably fit your body better than the smaller size you would usually buy.

Fig. 46. *A larger pattern size could bring darts and shoulder lines into position.*

Fig. 45. *Your back measurement can be too wide for the pattern piece.*

Small bra-cup sizes such as A or AA could call for a smaller pattern size if your shoulders are slim and/or narrow (Fig. 47). Choose the size that has the *most* measurements matching your own. This might be a pattern one size smaller than you would normally purchase. Your measurement chart will give you the answers. Pattern adjustments will probably involve the front-pattern segment only (when the proper size is chosen).

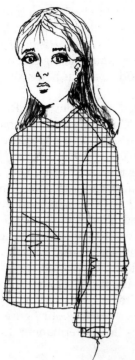

• *Rib Cage:* This alteration calls for a slight widening of the midsection of your usual size pattern and does not require a larger size.

• *Hip and Waistline:* Consider your hip and waistline dimensions when surveying a blouse pattern. A broad hipline and/or thick waistline will often call for alterations to a bodice pattern as well as the skirt pattern. You need more room in the lower portion of a blouse pattern (from just above the waistline to the hemline) to allow the bodice to button properly to the bottom edge. Fit the shoulders and bosom when choosing your bodice pattern, then make the necessary adjustments for the waistline/hipline areas. A broad hipline and/or thick waistline does not require a larger-size pattern.

• *Sleeve and Armhole:* Accommodating heavy arms includes readjusting the width of the sleeve and the set of the armhole (Fig. 48). This alteration does not require a larger size pattern.

Fig. 47. Try a smaller pattern size for a short, slender figure.

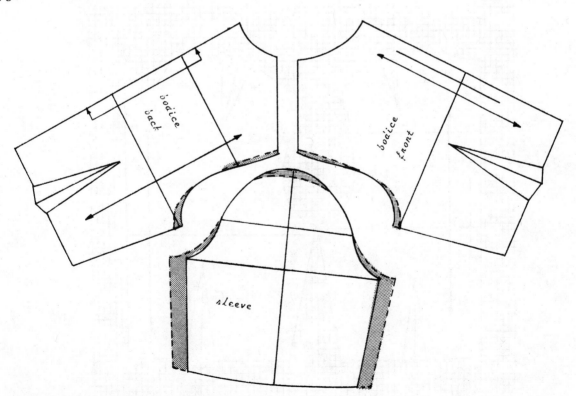

Fig. 48. Changing the size of the sleeves might involve armscye corrections, too.

41

Starting Your Sloper

Look through your pattern file before you decide to buy a new pattern; you might already have a shirt-style pattern that can be adjusted to meet your requirements. Don't hesitate over reusing a pattern because it was unsuccessful when it was made up the first time; any basic pattern requires personal fitting—that's what a sloper is all about.

Pattern Preparations

Press the pattern segments with a slightly warm iron to remove all creases. Pin the front-body segment of the bodice to your cutting board, aligning the center-front line with a vertical line on the board and the bottom point of the armhole opening on a horizontal line. If your cutting board is large enough, pin the back section in place next to the front, matching the armscyes along the same line (Fig. 49). Laying the pattern pieces on a grid makes measuring and resizing much easier. A view of the entire body pattern helps simplify the corrections.

Mark personal alterations directly on each pattern segment. Check the measurements on your assessment chart against the measurements on the envelope of the pattern. Correct each line that does not match your measurements.

You might find it easier to do the final alterations for your sloper on a muslin that can be tried on comfortably and altered without tearing. Cut the muslin from the partially personalized pattern segments using any sort of throwaway fabric. Leave a 1-inch seam allowance around each section of the pattern to provide room for additional alterations. Experiment with corrections to be sure you've chosen the best ones for your figure. Transfer the final alterations to a permanent form for your sloper.

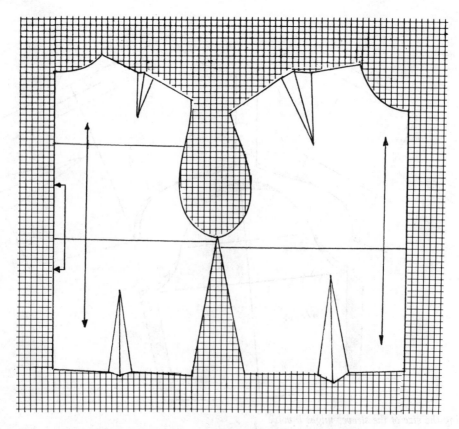

Fig. 49. Pin pattern segments to the cutting board.

Basic Corrections

TOO SNUG

Some pattern personalization is rather minor. It might only involve a snug feeling throughout the entire garment without involving any specific points. When the shoulder line and darts are correct, but the body of the pattern feels a tiny bit snug, there are two ways to make the correction:

1. When needed changes are less than 2 inches, the alterations can be made along the outside seam edges of the pattern without cutting the pattern or changing the basic design of the garment. Swing the side seams away from the center line (on front and/or back segments of the pattern) from armscye to the hemline (Fig. 50).

2. If the snugness includes the shoulder line or requires more than 2 inches of alteration, slash the pattern from shoulder to hem, through the vertical darts (Fig. 51). Spread the cut edges and insert a strip from shoulder to hemline to provide the wear-ease not provided within the pattern.

SHOULDER LINE

Since the point-of-fit for a blouse or dress pattern is the shoulder line, start personalizing the pattern from the top or shoulder line and work down to the hem. The entire garment, blouse or dress, hangs from the shoulder seams. Check the width and drop of the shoulder lines, both front and back. Indicate any alterations with a little dash or dot, but do not connect any lines until all corrections for the entire upper area are marked. New lines are graded to run smoothly into the original pattern lines wherever necessary.

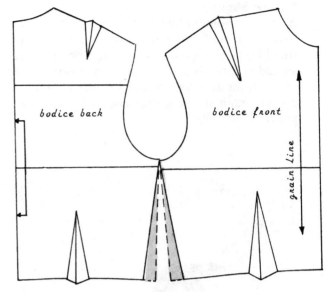

Fig. 50. Swing pattern side seams for a little extra ease.

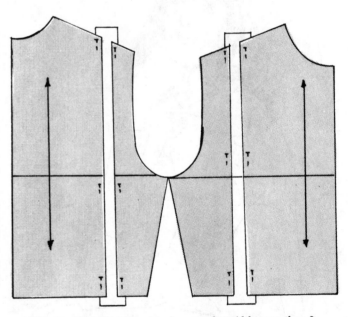

Fig. 51. Slash the pattern to increase the width more than 2 inches.

Narrow Shoulders

A narrow shoulder line often needs little attention beyond a pair of shoulder pads (Fig. 52). When the shoulder line drops below the outer point of your shoulder, it needs some raising. Pin a vertical dart in the front and back sections of the pattern top deep enough to bring the shoulder line up into position (Fig. 53).

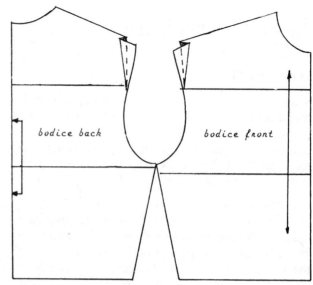

Fig. 53. Use a vertical dart to bring the shoulder line into position.

Measure the shoulder seam of the pattern and pin the darts perpendicular to the seam line, matching the pattern measurement with your own. This should clear up any wrinkles that appear at the armhole seam or the upper portion of the sleeve. Do not raise the line of the sleeve cap above the outer point of the shoulder or it will throw off the fit of the entire bodice. If the dart seems to shorten the armscye, redraw the opening to correct the problem.

Broad Shoulders

When the sleeve cap draws up over the top of your shoulder and/or the armscye feels as if it's choking you, the indication is that the shoulder line is too narrow for comfort (Fig. 54).

Add enough length to the shoulder line to meet your requirements. Slit the pattern and insert a wedge of tissue or fabric to accommodate the measurement of your shoulder (Fig. 55). Tape or pin the insert into place. Check the armhole to be sure you haven't changed the lines with your adjustments. If you have, redraw the portion of the armhole opening that was thrown off.

Fig. 52. Shoulder pads don't always take up enough slack.

44

Square Shoulders

Square shoulders will cause the bodice to wrinkle across the front and/or back between the bosom and neckline because there isn't enough fabric to accommodate the amount of natural shoulder padding (Fig. 56). Add a wedge parallel to the shoulder seam to spread the shoulder line of the pattern (Fig. 57). Readjust the sleeve cap to suit the new shoulder line.

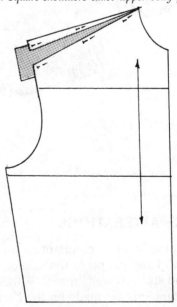

Fig. 54. Broad shoulders strain the lines of a shirt.

Fig. 56. Square shoulders cause upper body puckers.

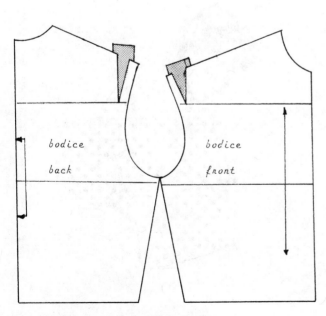

Fig. 55. Correction for broad shoulders.

Fig. 57. Spread the top of the pattern to your measurements.

Sloping Shoulders

The shoulder line needs to be raised if the pattern buckles below the armpit near the bustline darts (Fig. 58). A little wedge can be cut from the shoulder line, parallel to the seam (Fig. 59). This will smooth any ripples from the bodice. Check the armhole depth when making this adjustment; pulling up the shoulder line can also pull the armscye, taking away needed space. If this should occur, deepen the armscye to equal the amount you removed from the shoulder seam.

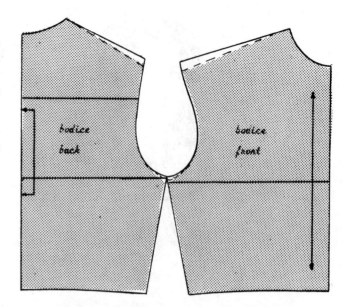

Fig. 59. Cut a wedge from the shoulder line to smooth the fit.

Fig. 58. A sloping shoulder line lets a garment sag.

BUSTLINE ALTERATIONS

Bustline fitting is very important to the finished appearance of any garment. You cannot have button-pull and still look well dressed. Although most bustline alterations are made on the front-pattern segment, the back, sleeve and armhole can also be involved.

Front Darts

Proper location of bustline darts is vital to the fit of the bodice. An underarm bustline dart starts at the side seam and ends in a point ½ inch from the peak of the bosom (Fig. 60).

Fig. 60. Locate underarm bustline darts properly.

Darts rising from the waistline end in a point approximately ½ inch to 1 inch below the peak of the bosom (Fig. 61).

Low Bustline

A low bustline, like a high one, calls for repositioning the bustline darts. With a low bustline, the darts on a commercial pattern are usually above the fullest part of the bosom (Fig. 63). Use the measurement from collarbone to apex. Drop the angle of the dart to meet the apex of the bosom. Be sure the point is properly located.

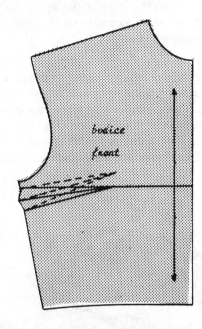

Fig. 62. Position darts for a high bosom.

Fig. 61. Example of waistline-to-bosom darts.

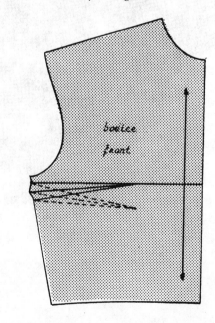

Fig. 63. Position darts for a low bosom.

High Bustline

If you have a high bustline, the angle of the darts will need adjusting to meet the apex of the bosom. When the bustline size needs no adjustment but the darts finish in the wrong place, compare your length from collarbone to apex of the bosom with that of the pattern. Also check the width across the bosom apex to identify the point or end of the dart. Relocate the angle of the dart according to your needs, from the side seam to the point of the dart (Fig. 62). Be sure the dart points directly to the apex of the bosom. Redraw the fold lines.

Small Cup Size

A small bosom (A- or AA-cup size) will usually cause puckering across the bustline of the bodice (Fig. 64). The correction for this problem is easier to make on the muslin when you can try on a garment.

Pin out the folds that appear on the bodice front between the neckline and bosom by taking a horizontal tuck across the muslin. Taper the tucks towards the side seams on each side (Fig. 65). Transfer the changes to your sloper.

Large Cup Size

If you wear a C-cup size or larger, and a pattern or finished garment normally pulls across the bustline, an H-shaped adjustment across the bosom of the pattern piece is the solution (Fig. 66). Again, you will find it easier to make the correction on the muslin, rather than on a paper-pattern segment.

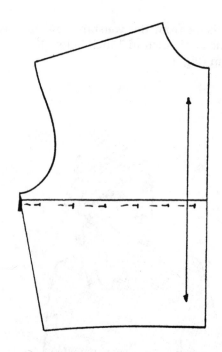

Fig. 65. Tuck the pattern to fit a small bosom.

Fig. 64. Bodice will buckle over small bosom.

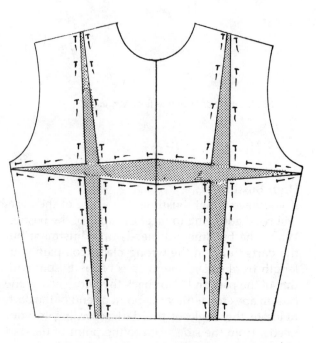

Fig. 66. Pattern corrections for fitting a large bosom.

48

Cut the pattern along the center of the darts horizontally, across the apex of the bosom vertically. Place an extra piece of fabric under the cut edges of the muslin, using the chart measurements as a guide. Spread the slashes until the pulls disappear and the bodice covers your bosom smoothly. Pin or tape the inset in place. When you rebaste the muslin, check the fit of the bosom area very carefully. Try on the muslin a second time to be sure you have allowed enough additional room for complete comfort and the proper hang of the bodice. Pin the dart lines directly on the muslin and redraw them after you check their positioning. Verify the fit of the armhole.

When making any bustline adjustments be doubly sure you've verified the placement of the darts and the armhole shaping. This final verification is a wise step; bustline changes can affect the depth and angle of the armhole opening, changing the set of your sleeve. Incomplete or incorrect adjustments could result in a poorly fitting sloper. Transfer the completed alterations to your sloper.

BACK

Occasionally, bustline alterations are made on the back segment of a pattern, rather than at the front. The B-cup figure who usually finds the bodice too snug (even though the pattern measurements seem right) should check the measurement across the back of the pattern against her personal measurement chart. The mirror will tell her that the pattern back is too narrow and where additional fabric is required (Fig. 67). The side seams pull towards the small segment of the pattern rather than hanging straight from armscye to waistline.

Broad Back

To eliminate the snugness of the upper part of the bodice, cut the muslin vertically, through the shoulder dart to a point slightly below the armscye at the line of the apex (Fig. 68). Pin or tape an additional strip of fabric under the opening, spreading the slash until the back feels comfortable when you move. Reset the shoulder darts.

Fig. 67. Check the fit of the pattern back.

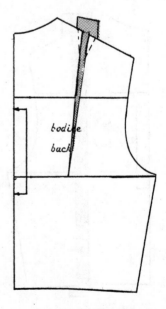

Fig. 68. Correction for back shoulder darts.

If the entire back segment of the pattern is too narrow, cut the pattern piece vertically and add a strip of fabric down the entire length (Fig. 69).

Narrow Back

A narrow back leaves too much fullness to gather unattractively at the back of a garment (Fig. 70). Excess fullness can be pinned out on the muslin. Create a vertical pleat from the center of the shoulder dart to the center of the waistline dart, easing out any unwanted fullness or puckering (Fig. 71). Redraw shoulder and waist darts.

POSTURE AND FIT

In addition to your physical contours, posture will affect the hang of a garment. When adjustments are not made to accommodate problems stemming from your posture, they show up most blatantly at the back of the finished garment.

Overly Straight

If you have perfect posture (a very straight back), you might find that a finished bodice buckles across the wing-bones (Fig. 72). Pin out any puckers that show up in the muslin and taper the pleat towards the side seams (Fig. 73).

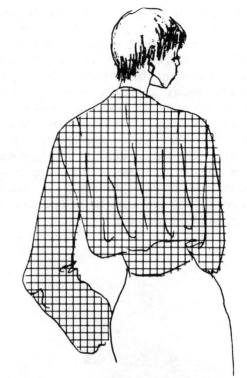

Fig. 70. The look of too much fabric at the back of the garment.

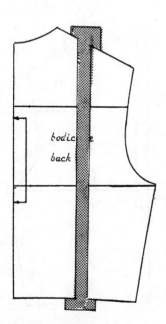

Fig. 69. Corrections for a too-narrow pattern back.

bodice back

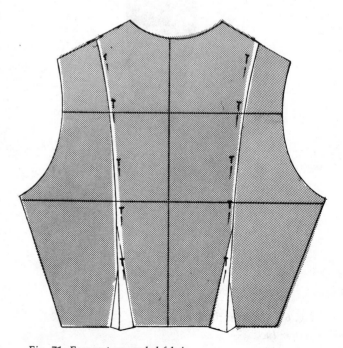

Fig. 71. Ease out unneeded fabric.

50

collar-gape by making a horizontal slash across the back of the muslin between the armhole seams to provide a little additional length above the shoulder blades (Fig. 75).

Insert a strip of fabric under the muslin and spread the slash until the neckline of the bodice snugs the top of the shoulder line, accommodates the roundness of the shoulder and allows the collar to return to its proper position. Tape or pin it to the fabric in place. If the fit of the neckline is too snug, cut a vertical slash and add a wedge of fabric under the muslin along the center back line. Recheck the fit before transferring these changes to your sloper.

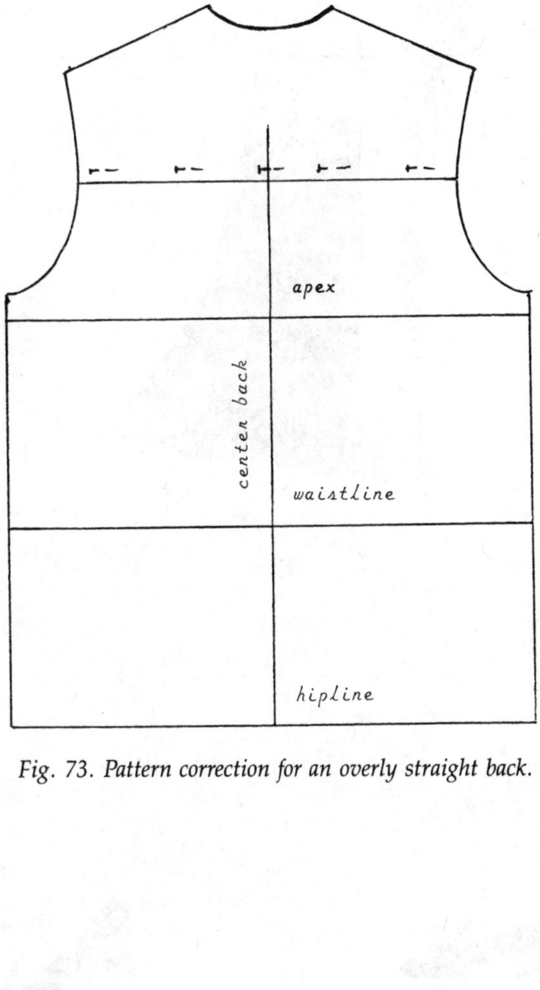

Fig. 73. Pattern correction for an overly straight back.

Fig. 72. Even perfect posture can cause fabric bunching.

Round Shoulders

Many women have what is commonly called a "dowager's hump." This roundness at the back across the shoulder line causes the collar to stand away from the nape of the neck and the shoulder seams to ride back on the body (Fig. 74). Correct

51

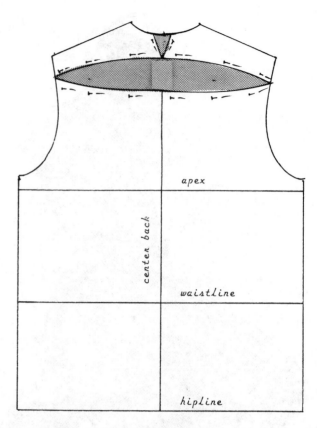

Fig. 75. *Correct collar-gape on a muslin.*

Labels in figure: *apex*, *center back*, *waistline*, *hipline*

Sleeves

There are three basic categories to consider when discussing sleeves:

1. A *set-in sleeve* is joined to the bodice with a seam that circles the arm around the peak of the shoulder (Fig. 76).

2. The *raglan sleeve* joins the bodice with a diagonal seam that stretches from the neckline to the underarm (Fig. 77).

3. *The kimono sleeve* is cut in one piece with the body of the garment (Fig. 78).

Fig. 74. *You can develop a "dowager's hump" at any age.*

Before you adjust the sleeve length be sure to verify the position of the elbow darts. These should not be ignored as properly placed elbow darts help the shaping and comfort of a long, fitted sleeve. The location of the elbow darts will also assist you in pinpointing the area for sleeve adjustments when they are necessary.

Fig. 76. The set-in sleeve.

Fig. 77. The raglan sleeve.

Fig. 78. The kimono sleeve.

POSITIONING SLEEVE DARTS

One Dart

To position a single dart correctly, allow your arm to hang loosely at your side, slightly bent. Direct the point of a single dart towards the center of the elbow (Fig. 79).

Two Darts

Two darts are always evenly spaced, on either side of the most prominent bone of the elbow (Fig. 80).

Three Darts

When the sleeve has three darts, the center dart is positioned the same as a single dart: pointing towards the center of the elbow. The other two darts are evenly spaced, on either side of the center dart (Fig. 81).

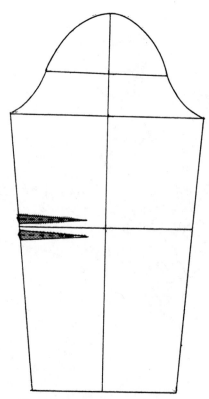

Fig. 80. Locating two sleeve darts.

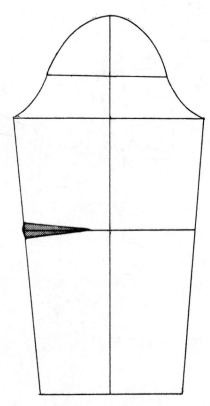

Fig. 79. Location of a single sleeve dart.

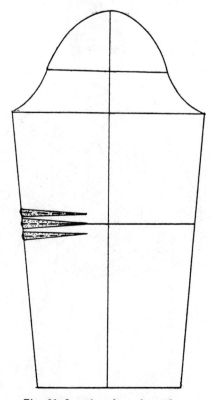

Fig. 81. Locating three sleeve darts.

SLEEVE LENGTH

Basic sleeve length is determined by the length of the arm (Fig. 82).

Cap Sleeve: A very short extension of the garment body. It usually does not continue through the armscye.

Short Sleeve: Covers the upper arm only. The length is approximately halfway from shoulder peak to elbow.

Elbow Length: Ends just at the top of the elbow completely covering the upper arm.

¾ Length: Hangs halfway between wrist and elbow.

⅞ Length: Ends just above the wristbone, halfway between ¾ length and a long sleeve.

Wrist Length: Sits just above the wristbone.

Long or *Full-Length Sleeve:* Completely covers the arm and wristbone ending at the top of the hand.

Use the appropriate measurement from your chart for the length of the sleeve. An inappropriate length spoils the effect of the entire garment. A sleeve that is too long will affect the shoulder seam. Constantly pushing up the cuff will cause the blouse to ride back pulling the shoulder and neck lines out of position.

If the sleeve is too short it will not only feel uncomfortable, it will destroy the fit of the shoulder line and pull the closure at the front.

PUCKERED SLEEVE TOP

Quite often, simply rearranging the placement of the ease around the sleeve cap will smooth out the puckers at the top of the sleeve (Fig. 83). This can be taken care of during the construction of the garment. Mark the sleeve pattern for the area of the sleeve cap that needs more gathering. The slanted puckering at the top of the sleeve will point towards the area that is short of fabric. The gathering should be fullest at that side. Rearrange the gathers of the sleeve as you sew.

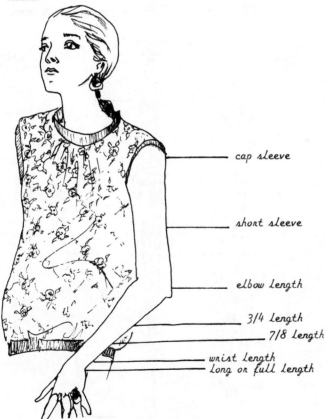

cap sleeve

short sleeve

elbow length

3/4 length

7/8 length

wrist length

long or full length

Fig. 82. CHART: Sleeve lengths.

Fig. 83. Rearrange gathers when sleeve top puckers.

Too Much Gathering

The average pattern has too much gathering for slender shoulders to fill. Flatten the top of the sleeve pattern, across the cap (Fig. 84).

Too Little Gathering

Where there never seems enough gathering around the top of a sleeve, enlarge the cap by raising the upper line of the sleeve. Cut the sleeve of the muslin across the cap and add a strip wide enough to produce the desired effect (Fig. 85). This will provide a little more fabric to cover the peak of the shoulder.

HEAVY ARMS

When a sleeve feels too tight down its entire length, slash the sleeve pattern vertically, along the grain line, and insert a strip of tissue from sleeve cap to wrist (Fig. 86). Grade the line of the sleeve cap to blend into the original cutting line. Lower the armhole to accommodate the additional fabric in the sleeve.

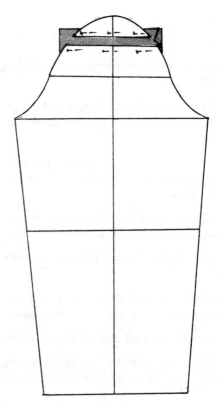

Fig. 85. Raise the sleeve top for additional fullness.

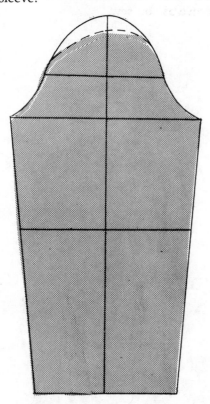

Fig. 84. Flatten the sleeve top for less fullness.

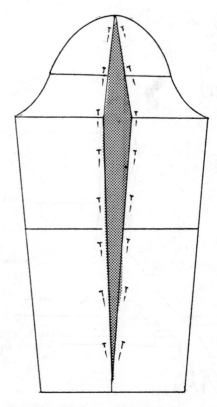

Fig. 86. Widen the sleeve with a slash along the grain line.

Upper-Arm Adjustments

The upper-arm area might be the only place that the sleeve doesn't fit properly. This type of correction is very common for the more mature woman. It is handled by slashing the upper part of the sleeve and does not require any adjustment to the lower segment.

Slash the sleeve pattern parallel to the grain line and insert a wedge from the top of the sleeve cap to just below the elbow (Fig. 87). Redraw the armhole opening of the bodice to accommodate the new width at the top of the sleeve.

THIN ARMS

If the entire sleeve wrinkles from too much fabric, pin out the excess by taking a vertical pleat along the grain line, from sleeve cap to wrist (Fig. 88).

Where the sleeve is too wide in the upper or lower portion only, taper the pleat to include only the area that is too wide; stop just above or below the portion that fits properly (Fig. 89).

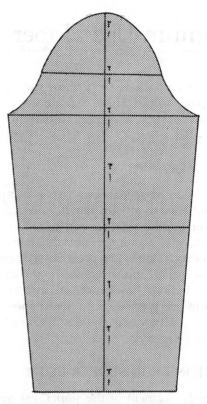

Fig. 88. Tuck the pattern to fit thin arms.

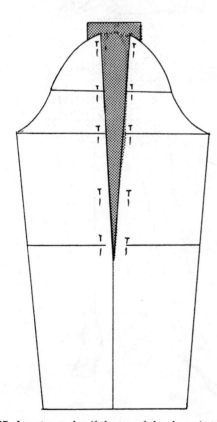

Fig. 87. Insert a wedge if the top of the sleeve is too tight.

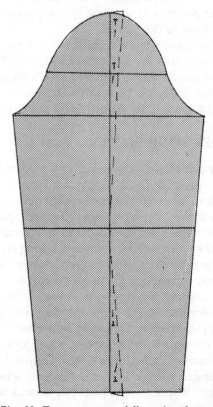

Fig. 89. Taper out excess fullness in select areas.

57

Maximum-Use Sloper

Make written notations for pattern variations directly on your sloper. That's the one way you can keep pattern designs and great ideas from getting away.

SLEEVE VARIATIONS

Sleeve-and-cuff variations can give a completely new appearance to an old, familiar pattern. Note the measurements for a banded cuff, fitted cuff, French cuff, and/or gauntlet, directly on the sleeve segment of your sloper. List potential style changes and always include measurements to put each one into effect. Indicate how much length is added to cut a cuff in one piece with the sleeve, how much length is subtracted to cut the sleeve elbow-length, short or as a cap style.

VARIATIONS FOR SLOPER BODY

On the body segment of the sloper, list neckline changes that will work for your pattern. Create new collar patterns. Draft them on a separate sheet and clip them to the sloper.

Mark the upper-body section for various yoke locations and note the number of inches added to the side seams for a full, gathered smock style. See the chapter titled "Be Your Own Designer" (page 91) for additional ideas on extended pattern use.

IDENTIFY YOUR SLOPER

Label the completed sloper with the current date, your measurements and weight, and the *name* of each pattern piece: *bodice front, bodice back, sleeve,* etc. This makes it easy to identify each pattern piece when you want to reuse it or to identify the pieces if they are folded for storage. Dating is also a gentle reminder of the time to recheck your sloper dimensions or readjust for weight changes.

When refitting an outdated sloper, be sure to mark it *corrected*, along with the date and other pertinent information. This is an important record for your pattern. Knowing when your sloper was brought current, when it was last adjusted, and what changes were made can tell you whether your sloper is usable or whether it should be resized before use.

While weight changes of 5 to 10 pounds affect the fit of the pattern, time and gravity will also cause changes (Fig. 90). They can change the hang and location of the waistline, hemline, and/or the sleeve. Always check the measurements of an old sloper before cutting into your fabric.

Fig. 90. Refit your sloper when clothing doesn't look or feel right.

Treat your sloper as you would any personal treasure. Hang it in the closet for storage or roll it carefully and store it in a large mailing tube. Care for it and it will care for you.

When you buy new commercial patterns, open each piece and press with a warm iron to remove the creases. Place the bodice sections of the pattern on top of your sloper. Carefully compare the lines you customized to match your body measurements with the outlines of the commercial pattern. Trace the corrections from the sloper to the commercial pattern for a personalized fit of all new designs. The ease with which you achieve perfection for your completed garments will bring a new excitement to your personal sewing.

DRAFTING A SKIRT SLOPER

Instead of matching your waistline to the measurements on the envelope of the skirt pattern you choose for conversion to a sloper, match the hipline measurement. Skirt patterns require fewer alterations when the hipline measurement of a commercial pattern comes close to your own. It gives you a head start towards your completed personal pattern (Fig. 91).

Start your personal adjustments at the top of each pattern segment and work your way down to the hem. Take each area in progression to keep from missing any necessary corrections.

When to Cut a Muslin

You will probably be able to complete your adjustments on the tissue-paper pattern segments if they don't go much beyond moving a few cutting lines (Fig. 92). If your alterations are complicated and/or extensive, you might find that cutting a "muslin" will be a big help. A muslin is a fabric pattern that can be tried on and altered repeatedly without fear of tearing; it does not have to be made of muslin

Fig. 91. A good sloper means good results.

but can be cut from any inexpensive pre-shrunk fabric. (In the U.K. "muslin" is known as "calico.") One-inch-square checkered gingham works very well and even offers a bonus: The squares define a rough measurement and location for your alterations.

Transfer your personal corrections to the muslin; machine-baste the fabric together and try it on to finalize cutting lines and darts. Any additional alterations can be made at this time. Mistakes are never transferred to the sloper.

It is a good idea to hang your fitted muslin in the closet or fold and store it in a drawer after use, particularly if your weight changes easily. It is reusable for future fittings or alterations. You can even keep it in a large manila envelope or plastic bag at the back of your pattern file. If you suddenly realize that the fit of your clothes has gone a little astray, take out your muslin, press out any creases and try it on again. Make the new corrections, transfer the new lines to your sloper and, again, store your muslin for additional use.

Waist and Hipline

Width adjustments of *less* than 2 inches can be handled along the outside seam lines without making any changes to the center part of the pattern (Fig. 93). This is the simplest form of pattern adjustment.

- *To widen the pattern:* Tape an extra strip of tissue or pattern paper outside any areas that need widening. Mark the alteration outside the cutting line.

- *To decrease the pattern width:* Mark the amount inside the stitching line. Draw the new cutting line parallel to the existing one, grading the new cutting line to flow into the original line.

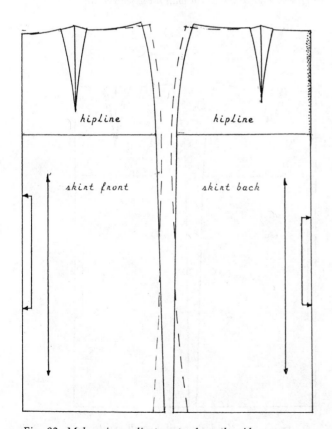

Fig. 92. Make minor adjustments along the side seams.

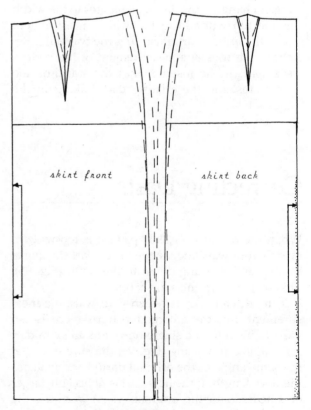

Fig. 93. Simple pattern adjustments.

Increasing Pattern Dimensions

Widening a skirt *more* than 2 inches requires slashing the pattern. By cutting down the length of the skirt you do not alter the original style of the pattern; the necessary width is added within the seam lines (Fig. 94.) Redraw darts to conform with your waistline measurements.

- Check your high and low hip measurements to be sure that the addition you plan for the hipline of the pattern is adequate.

- Cut the pattern from waistline to hem outside the dart closest to the seam edge. Spread the pattern to the width of your hipline measurement and place a strip of pattern paper or tissue underneath the cut edges of the pattern piece. When the adjustment is right, pin or tape the strip in place.

- Altering the hipline of a skirt often involves moving or changing the dart(s). Changes to the width at the hip will add to the width measurement over the entire skirt, including the waistline. Recheck the waistline measurement of the pattern segment. If the insert makes the waistline too large, reshape the existing darts taking in the excess fabric.

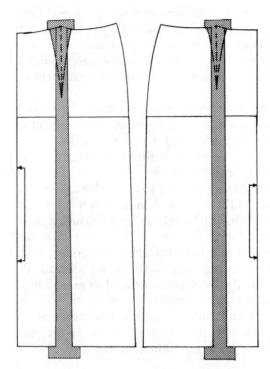

Fig. 94. Add to the width within the pattern lines.

Correcting Darts

When the top of your skirt pattern is too wide to ever fit your waistline, deepen each dart starting at the top and working down to the point (Fig. 95). This will take up the extra fabric.

If the discrepancy between your waistline measurement and the enlarged pattern piece is too great to include in a single dart, add an extra dart for shaping and sizing (Fig. 96). Be sure it falls at the same angle as the original dart(s) and matches them for length. If the new dart is noticeably larger or smaller than the original one(s), readjust the size of all darts to make them equal.

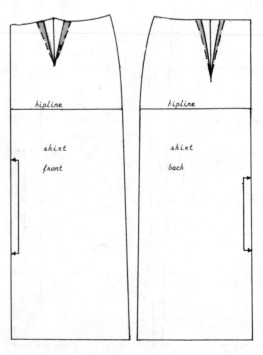

Fig. 95. Deepen the darts to fit a small waistline.

Widening the Waist and/or Hips

Occasionally, we find the hipline fits perfectly but the waistline needs a little additional room. This can be handled in one of two ways:

1. Make the darts narrower putting more material into use across the top of the skirt (Fig. 97)

2. Cut the outside seam line a little straighter from the widest part of the hip to the top (Fig. 98). These are both simple changes; either one can do the job.

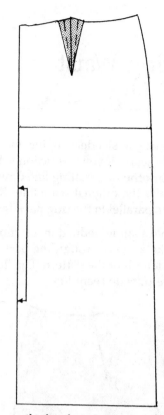

Fig. 97. Narrow the dart for more room at the waistline.

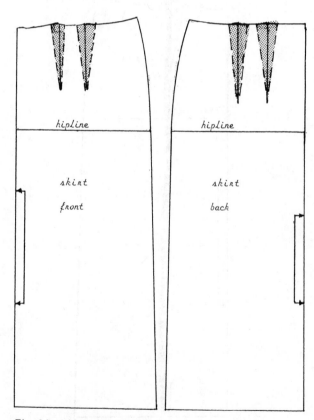

Fig. 96. Add a second dart when necessary.

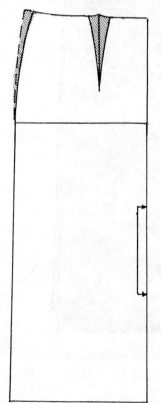

Fig. 98. Cut the upper portion of the skirt a little wider.

Reducing Waist and/or Hips

- Accommodate a slender hipline by redrawing the outside seam, if your reduction is less than 2 inches. Mark the new cutting line directly on the pattern *inside* the original seam line. Redraw the cutting line parallel to the original edge (Fig. 99).

- For a hip/waistline reduction of more than 2 inches, take a pleat through the dart and down the entire length of the pattern (Fig. 100). Do not disturb the outside seam line.

- Start at the waistline and fold a pleat down the length of the pattern segment to the hem. Tape or pin the pleat in place.

- Check the waistline to be sure it will still fit properly. Commercial patterns have approximately 10 inches (differential) between waist and hip measurements.

- Redraw the dart(s) at the top of the skirt if necessary.

- If your hipline is particularly narrow in comparison to your waistline, taper the tuck from the top of the skirt to the hemline. Leave a little more room at the waist: Deepen the tuck towards the hem. This will wedge the reduction and prevent bagging from hipline to hem.

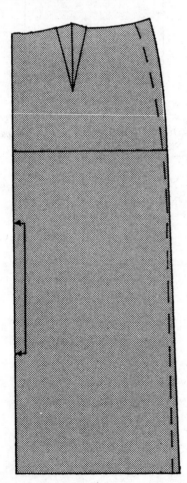

Fig. 99. Draw a new seam line inside the pattern edge.

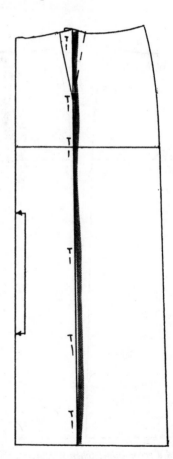

Fig. 100. Pleat the pattern for a major reduction.

Protruding Stomach

When the front of the skirt rides up over a protruding stomach, puckering the hipline and/or pulling the hemline, you need a little more room at the center front of your skirt (Fig. 101). It is easier to make adjustments for a protruding stomach or a swayback on a muslin rather than the flat paper pattern.

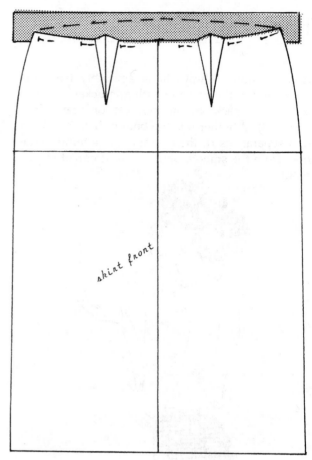

Fig. 102. Corrections for a protruding stomach.

- Drop the center front of the skirt until the hemline is hanging straight across.

- Add an extra strip of fabric to the pattern, anywhere from ¼ inch to 2 inches depending upon the roundness of the stomach. Tape or pin the material along the upper edge, parallel to the waistline, to fill in the gap to the waist (Fig. 102). Taper the insert towards the side seams.

- Correct the placement of the darts and transfer the new markings to your sloper.

Fig. 101. With the right corrections the skirt hangs straight.

Back Adjustments

A skirt should always hang smoothly from the waistband to the hemline with no puckers or pulls across the back, at the pockets or seam lines (Fig. 103). Whether it is the bottom half of a dress or a separate skirt, there should be nothing to detract from the smooth drape of the completed garment.

Fig. 103. The back of the skirt should not pucker.

Swayback

The alteration for swayback or very rounded buttocks is handled at the back of the skirt, just under the waistband. You will find it easier and more accurate to make this correction on a muslin.

• Raise the center back until no wrinkles appear across the top of the buttocks. Pin the wedge out of the muslin tapering towards either side (Fig. 104). Shorten the darts to prevent them from creating new pulls across the back of the skirt.

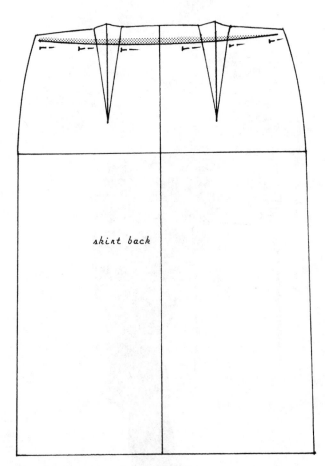

Fig. 104. Corrections for a swayback.

Flat Buttocks

Occasionally the skirt back puckers, not from the roundness of the buttocks, but because of a very flat bottom (Fig. 105). The adjustment for this pattern correction starts at the same place as the swayback alteration, just below the waistline. It is a two-part alteration (Fig. 106).

- Cut away ¼ inch or more across the center back below the waistline to make the hem hang straight. The remainder of the correction is a vertical one.

- Make a vertical pleat starting at the top of the skirt and taper it to the hemline. The depth of the tuck will depend upon how much excess fabric must be eased out of the skirt. For two inches or less, one pleat down the center should result in a neatly fitted skirt back. Alterations of more than 2 inches require a pleat at each side, through the center of the dart to the hemline.

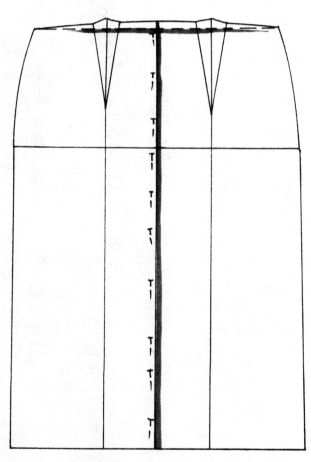

Fig. 106. The two-part alteration to fit a flat bottom.

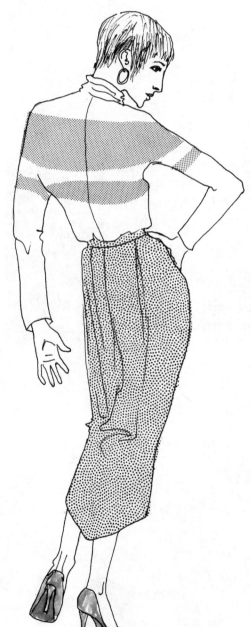

Fig. 105. A flat buttocks lets the skirt back sag.

Length

Measure the length of the pattern and correct to your preferred length. This is particularly important when you make pattern alterations. Extensive alterations to the width can noticeably change the length of the skirt (Fig. 107). Remeasure the hem allowance for uniformity; correct if necessary.

Marking for Added Use

In addition to your normal street length, measure and mark your skirt sloper for any other lengths that you might use. This would include tennis skirts, golf skirts, ice-skating costumes, evening gowns, cocktail dresses, etc. (Fig. 108).

Fig. 107. Check your hemline.

Measure for each additional length and draw the hemlines completely across the pattern. Identify each marking. When using the sloper for an alternate length, fold under that section of the pattern not in use. Do not cut into your sloper to effect style changes.

Finalizing Your Sloper

Check all seams before transferring your corrections to a permanent form. Make sure that everything is complete with new lines graded to meet existing pattern lines, sew lines indicated for all darts and construction information correct for all personal adjustments.

Trace your pattern lines—seams, darts, hems,

etc.—to nonwoven fabric or heavy interfacing. Transfer all construction details you will need to the sloper. Bond the pattern to an additional length of nonwoven fabric for strength and permanence. Tagboard or other lightweight cardboard is also a good base for your slopers.

On either the front or back segment of your sloper, write your true waistline measurement and the measurements for waistbands with a closure and without: button or hook band; drawstring band. Note that the waistband *with* closure should be interfaced.

For ideas on extending the use of your skirt sloper (creating new fashions) see "Be Your Own Designer" (page 91). You will find additional drawings, creative ideas and information to assist you in designing your own clothing and recycling existing patterns.

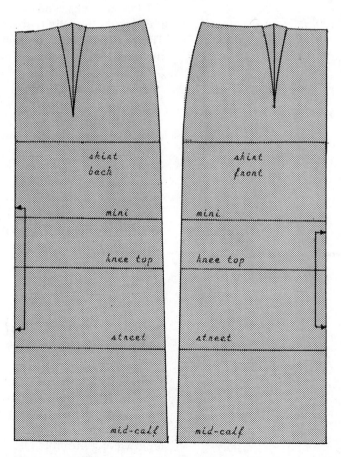

Fig. 108. Mark all usable lengths on the pattern.

CREATING A PERSONAL SLOPER: PANTS

Fig. 109. A good fit is vital.

Commercial pants patterns require more personal adjustments than any other type of pattern you use. Even when the measurements on the pattern envelope *appear to* match closely with your own, pants cut from that pattern rarely fit the way they should. Pattern companies lean towards average sizing and ignore critical points-of-fit: high or low rise, adjustments for a round or flat stomach, full or slim buttocks, wide or narrow hips, and most important, the actual shaping of the crotch line. The result is that a commercial pant pattern is almost useless as it comes from the envelope.

On the positive side, the general lines of a commercial pant pattern can be used to shape your sloper. Simply borrow the shape of the pattern and merge it with your personal measurements. Compare the measurements on the pattern envelope with your personal chart and select the pattern with the measurements closest to your hipline dimensions (Fig. 109).

At some point in your sewing career you may have had a pants sloper made that didn't really fulfil its promise. This is the time to take it out, correct all existing errors and make it into a working personal pattern.

How Pants Fit

Front and back segments of a pants pattern are not identical (Fig. 110). The back of the pattern has more width across the buttocks and hips than the front-pattern segment. There is also additional length along the crotch line from the center back to the inseam. These extra inches are required for the back segment of the pattern if the body is to bend at the hips or achieve a seated position comfortably. In addition, the line of the crotch must be properly drawn to conform to the actual shape of the body. The crotch line is the prime line-of-fit for a pair of pants.

The complete crotch line (including both rises and the crotch bed) is shaped somewhat like a "U" that has been bumped out at the bottom.

The front rise starts from the center of the waistline. It curves gently down and under the body (the crotch bed) and continues at a gentle slope, down and back to meet the inseam.

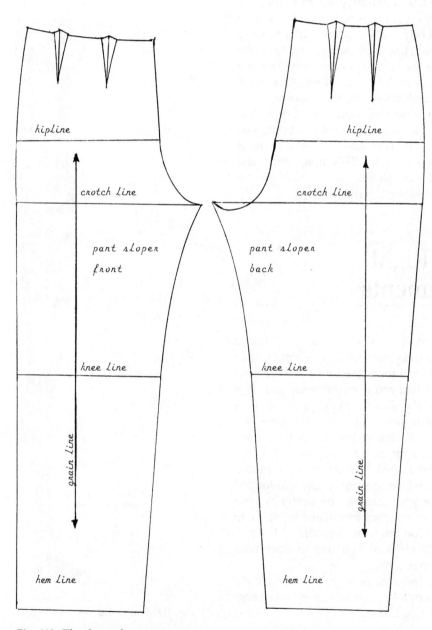

Fig. 110. The shape of a pants pattern.

On the back-pattern section, the rise starts at the center back of the waistline, angles down to the buttocks, curves down and around the buttocks, falls below the crotch bed at the lowest point and rises slowly towards the front to meet the inseam line at the center of the body.

Where commercial patterns fail is in the area of the crotch *bed* or base. The curve does not drop low enough at the back to adequately accommodate the buttocks, nor does it curve properly in front to fit the curve of the body and allow the pants to hang correctly. The crotch line is the most important correction to change the standard (average) lines of a commercial pattern to the personal measurements and shape you need for your pants sloper.

Once you are aware of how the crotch line should be shaped to properly meet the body, you will have a perfect fit every time you sew a pair of pants—whatever the style. This line, front and back rises plus the crotch bed, is the most important shaping in drafting a pants pattern.

Use the Right Measurements

When you took your measurements, you started with a string around your middle to identify your natural waistline. You then attached a second cord at the center back that you drew between your legs and secured at the front, allowing it to pass through the crotch area (Fig. 111). This gave you the measurement for the entire crotch line: front and back rises plus the crotch bed.

From the second cord you dropped a plumb line. The point at which the plumb line was looped is the location for your inseam, the center of your body. The number of inches from your waistline to the inseam point (on the front segment of the pattern), is the measurement you use to start your pants pattern corrections.

Select your pattern, make sure it is completely free from creases or folds and secure the front segment to your cutting board.

Fig. 111. Proper measurements shape your pants sloper.

Pattern Front

LINE-OF-FIT

Start at the top of the pattern front and measure the crotch line from the waist to the inseam. Set a flexible metal or heavy, plastic-coated fabric tape measure on edge along the crotch rise and curve it to include the entire length of the front crotch (Fig. 112). Compare this measurement with the measurement of your chart. The length of the line on the pattern will probably vary from what you actually need. If the line of the pattern is longer than your front-crotch measurement, mark the correction directly on the pattern, inside the inseam line (Fig. 113).

In most cases, the crotch line of the pattern will be shorter than your own measurement from waistline to inseam. This is the most common error of a commercial pattern rarely fit as hoped. A short crotch bed will cause the pants to ride up when you walk, cut through the crotch area and pull down at the center of the waistband.

To add to the length of the crotch bed, tape pattern tissue to the crotch bed/inseam area and extend the lines to match the measurements indicated on your chart (Fig. 114).

The next step is to correct any fitting errors in the body of the pants pattern.

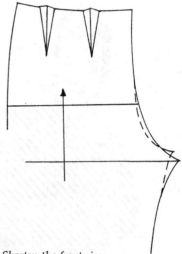

Fig. 113. Shorten the front rise.

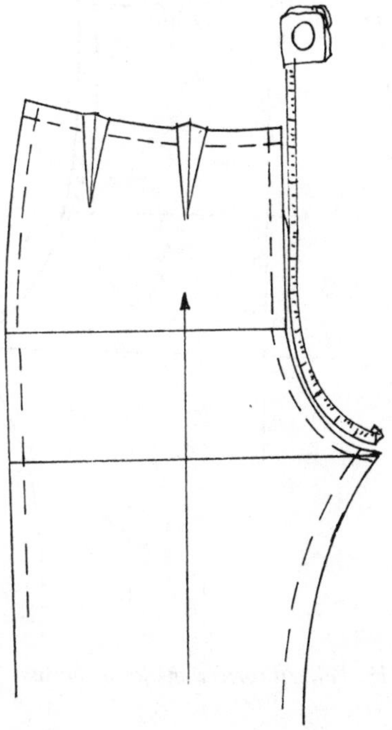

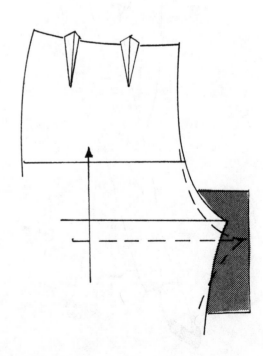

Fig. 112. Measure the front rise.

Fig. 114. Lengthen the front rise.

CONCAVE OR FLAT STOMACH

A flat or even slightly concave stomach leaves too much unneeded fabric to gather unattractively at the front of your slacks between your hip bones (Fig. 115).

Indication: Excess fabric at front bunching across the crotch and upper thigh because the front segment of the pattern is too wide for your body.

Correction: Straighten the line of the center-front rise from the waist to the beginning of the crotch-bed curve (Fig. 116). If this correction is not enough to eliminate the gathers, lower the waistline slightly, tapering the line towards the sides.

PROTRUDING STOMACH

A protruding stomach requires a little additional fabric across the front of the pants (Fig. 117).

Indication: Pockets pull and front puckers along side seam.

Correction: This correction is easier to make on a muslin but you can start it on the flat pattern. Add a wedge parallel to front rise (Fig. 118). Pin or tape an additional strip at the top of the pattern and extend the waistline up ¼ to ½ inch (depending upon the roundness of your stomach). When you try on the muslin, make sure that the side seams hang straight up and down and the grain of the fabric is even across your body.

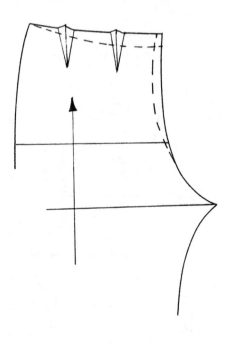

Fig. 116. Pattern corrections for a concave stomach.

Fig. 115. Excess fabric spoils the look of your pants.

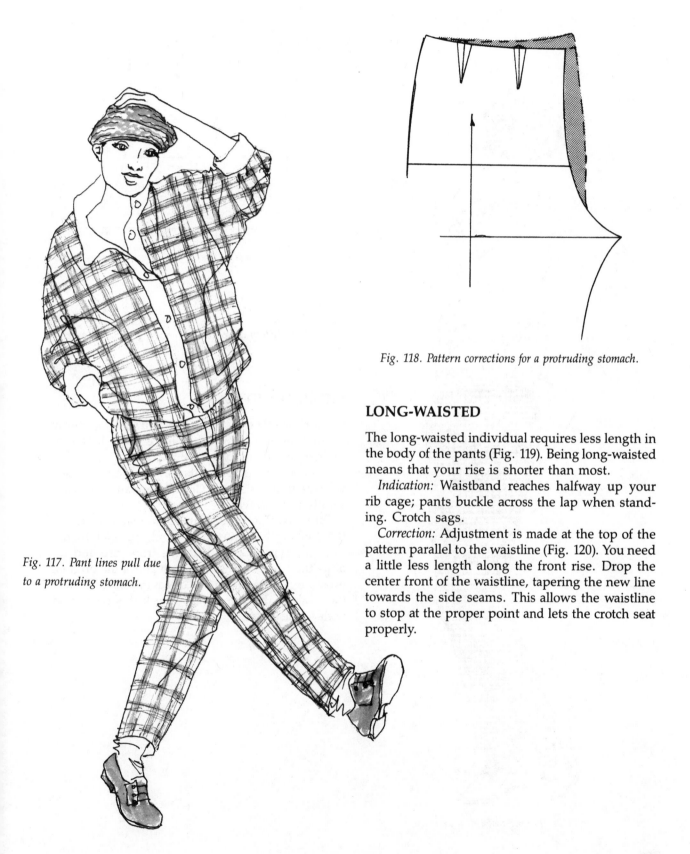

Fig. 118. Pattern corrections for a protruding stomach.

LONG-WAISTED

The long-waisted individual requires less length in the body of the pants (Fig. 119). Being long-waisted means that your rise is shorter than most.

Indication: Waistband reaches halfway up your rib cage; pants buckle across the lap when standing. Crotch sags.

Correction: Adjustment is made at the top of the pattern parallel to the waistline (Fig. 120). You need a little less length along the front rise. Drop the center front of the waistline, tapering the new line towards the side seams. This allows the waistline to stop at the proper point and lets the crotch seat properly.

Fig. 117. Pant lines pull due to a protruding stomach.

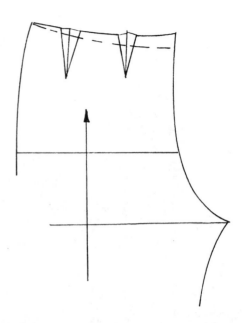

Fig. 120. Pattern corrections for the long-waisted figure.

SHORT-WAISTED

If your waistline is very high you are constantly running into the problem of not enough length to the rise of a pants pattern (Fig. 121).

Indication: Waist of pants never seems to reach your natural waistline. Crotch line cuts and constantly pulls down.

Correction: Pin or tape an additional strip across the top of the pattern segment, parallel to the waistline (Fig. 122). Extend the front rise and redraw the waist ¼ inch to ¾ inch above the original waistline, tapering the line out at the sides to meet the peak of the side seam. Check this correction with a muslin.

Fig. 119. The long-waisted figure.

WAISTLINE

Check the waistline measurement of the pattern. Where changes are necessary, include the width of the dart(s) with the waistline measurement and mark the adjustments directly on the pattern before you continue. A pattern that does not fit properly at the waist can be altered according to the directions given for adjusting the waistline of a skirt (see "Drafting a Skirt Sloper," page 60).

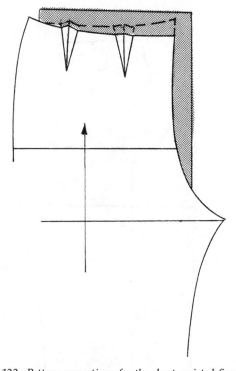

Fig. 122. Pattern corrections for the short-waisted figure.

Fig. 121. The short-waisted figure.

HIPLINE

Compare your high and low hipline measurements with the pattern. If the pattern is too wide, indicate your measurements on the pattern within the side seams for the narrower lines you require (Fig. 123). Measure from the center-front rise towards the outside seam edge.

Add pattern tissue along the outside seam edge if it is necessary to widen the pattern at the hipline (Fig. 124).

LEGS

Don't overlook the leg width of the pants pattern. Creating a baggy look is one thing; unintentionally baggy pant legs are entirely different. Accidentally baggy pant legs are as unacceptable as overly tight pant legs. Compare the measurements on your personal chart with the measurements on the pattern envelope and adjust accordingly.

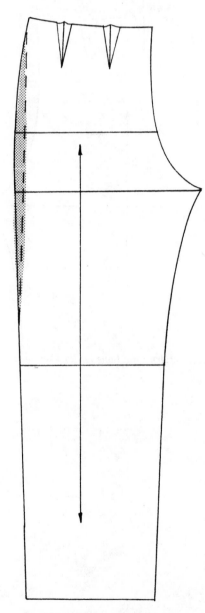

Fig. 123. Narrowing the hipline.

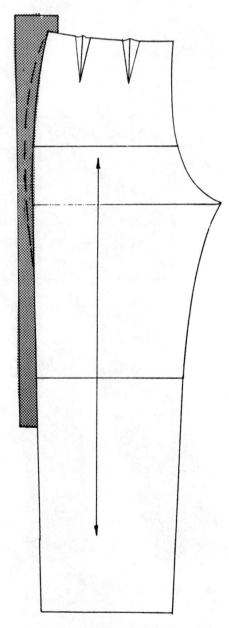

Fig. 124. Widening the hipline.

SLENDER LEGS

Pant legs are narrowed to accommodate slender thighs and knees (Fig. 125). The measurement of your thigh should be compared to the measurement of the pant leg. Eliminate the extra fabric by tapering the leg of the pattern.

Redraw the curve of the inseam line from the crotch bed to meet any new points you mark along the upper leg of the pattern along the inseam and the outside seam edge.

HEAVY LEGS

Heavy thighs and/or knees need a little extra room in the upper portion of the pant leg to keep the fabric smooth. Add tissue along the outer edges of the pattern and redraw the lines to meet your needs (Fig. 126). Grade all new seam lines to flow smoothly into the original pattern lines.

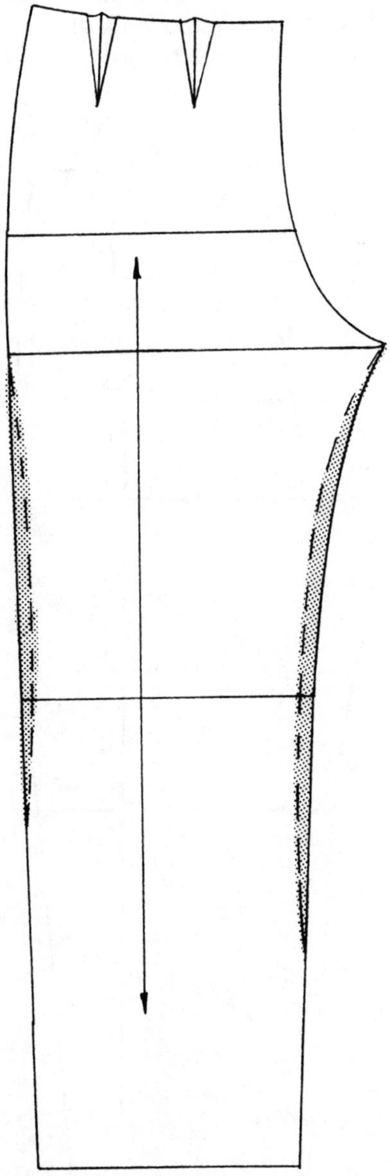

Fig. 125. Slimming pant legs.

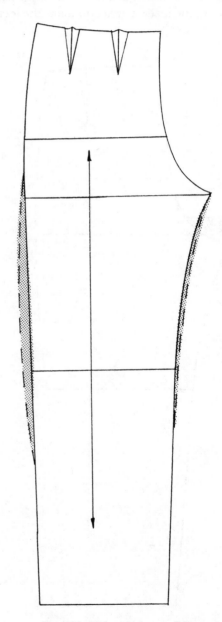

Fig. 126. Widen the legs to fit.

79

PATTERN BACK

Start the corrections for the back half of the pattern from the crotch line. Measure the back rise and crotch bed carefully using the same methods employed for the front corrections.

CROTCH-FITTING

Measure the back-crotch line as you did for the front segment of the pattern. For most figures, the back-crotch line will be too short. Tape pattern tissue along the inseam area and mark the location for the new crotch line (Fig. 127). Be sure the back-crotch bed conforms to the shape of your body.

A few of you will find the back-crotch line too long. To shorten the back-crotch length, measure the pattern as you did for the front segment and correct the drawing to match your needs (Fig. 128).

CROTCH BED

Review the contour of the crotch curve. Be sure that the line at the bottom back of the curve falls *below* the line of the crotch bed.

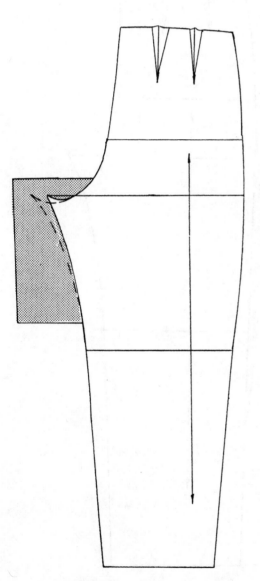

Fig. 127. Reshape crotch lines to meet your body.

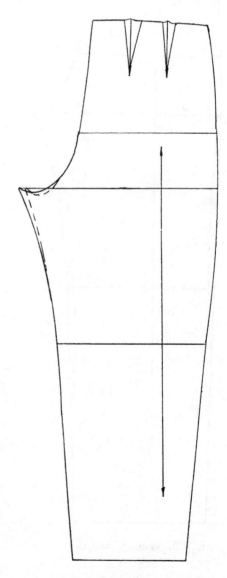

Fig. 128. Shorten the crotch back.

A low-hanging posterior might need as much as a 2-inch drop below the crotch bed; the average is approximately ½ to 1 inch. This correction provides room for the pants to seat properly against the body, prevents the crotch seam from riding up and cutting and provides enough back length to keep the waistline in place when you sit down. Don't overcorrect the drop; it should fit to the shape of your body, not hang below. When you try on the corrected pattern or muslin you can readjust this line if necessary.

LARGE BUTTOCKS

Very rounded buttocks or broad hips require some space beyond that created by dropping the crotch bed. Ease the width along the body of the pattern to better accommodate your measurements.

Indication: Crotch pulls up, waistline pulls down when seated. There is visible pulling along the side seams and pockets.

Correction: Lengthen the center back rise by raising the waistline ¼ inch at a time until a proper depth is reached (Fig. 129). Add to the side seam from the waistline to below the hipline. If the fit still isn't quite right, deepen the crotch curve to allow pants to seat properly against buttocks. Shorten the back darts slightly to prevent future pull.

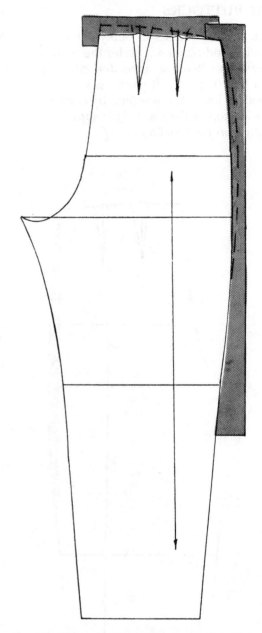

Fig. 129. Pattern back corrections for broad buttocks.

FLAT BUTTOCKS

Indication: Fabric falls in bulky gathers from the waistline and pants sag under the buttocks.

Correction: Remove unneeded curve from side seam line (Fig. 130). If pants back still doesn't lie smoothly, lower the waistline by cutting ¼" to ¾" from the top of the waist. This adjustment is best handled on the muslin.

Swayback

Indication: Bunching of fabric across top of buttocks at small of back.

Correction: Pants and skirts take the same type of alteration (Fig. 131). (See "Skirts: Adjustment for Swayback," page 66) Pin a horizontal pleat across small of back to remove the excess fabric below the back waistline. Shorten the darts to prevent the same type of fabric pull from recurring.

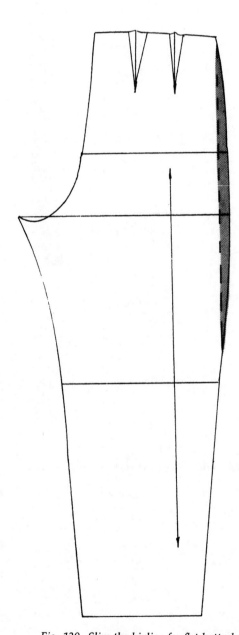

Fig. 130. Slim the hipline for flat buttocks.

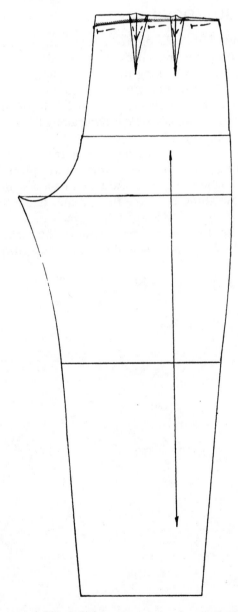

Fig. 131. Pattern correction for swayback.

Legs: Back

Correct the thigh width if necessary. Puckers or ripples will point to the area that requires alteration. Front and back segments of a pants pattern are not the same width and don't necessarily take the same amount of adjustment. It totally depends on your personal measurements.

Loose Upper Legs

Indication: Too much fabric clumping at sides of thigh area.
  Correction: Taper along side seam until leg looks right (Fig. 132).

Tight Upper Legs

Indication: Not enough fabric from low hip to knee, legs pull at seam lines.
  Correction: Add a tapered wedge along the side seam to widen area (Fig. 133).

Length

Compare the length of the pattern leg with the measurements on your personal chart. Make whatever corrections are necessary. When changing the length of your pants, don't forget to redraw the hem facing at the bottom of the leg.

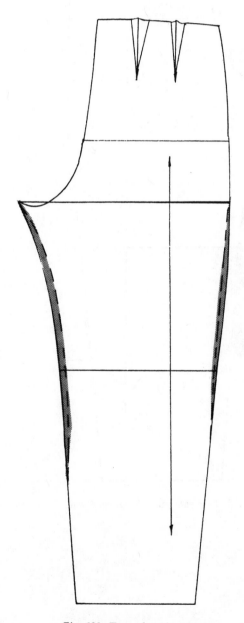

Fig. 132. Taper the side seams.

83

Final Pattern Fitting

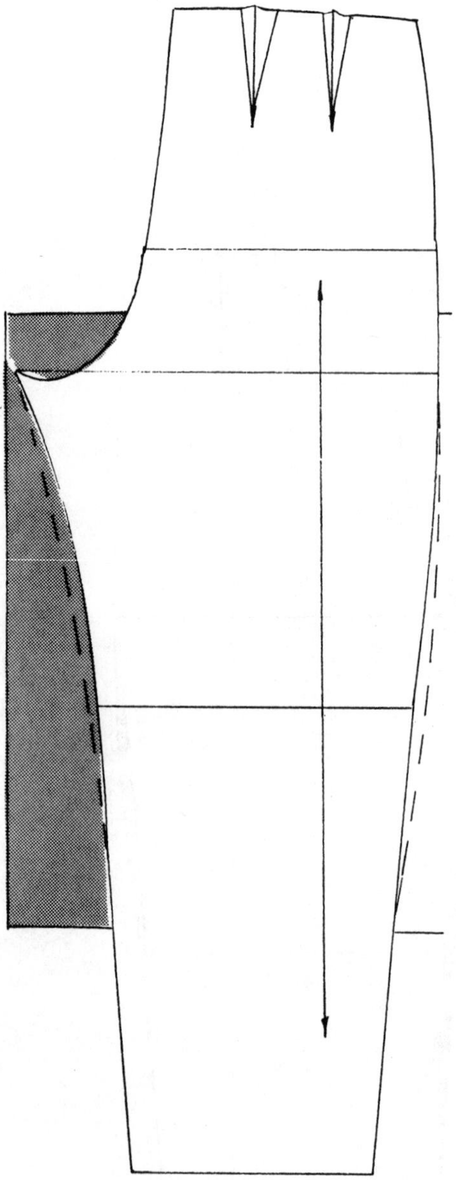

You've read this before: Proper fitting is critical to the finished look of a pair of pants. There is no place you can hide any fitting errors on the finished garment. Don't *assume* that the corrected pattern is perfect because you followed your measurement chart. Test the corrections you made on the flat pattern by cutting a muslin. Finalize all lines on the muslin before cutting into expensive fabric. If some additional adjustments are necessary, a muslin is the perfect place to make them.

Use your muslin as an artist uses a canvas. Draw on it, make notes on it or mark it for adjustments and alternate views. Cut away unnecessary fabric if the muslin is too loose; sew or tape in additional pieces if you think an area is too tight. Machine-baste scraps of fabric to the muslin to achieve the length and width you require, but be sure to maintain the grain lines between the fabric and sewn-in scraps to retain the integrity of the fit.

Try on the test pants (the muslin) as many times as necessary to achieve the fit you desire. When the muslin fits and feels the way you want (no additional alterations necessary), it is the time to put the results into the most permanent form possible.

Bond the tissue to interfacing or nonwoven fabric or trace your pattern onto tagboard. Another option is to use the muslin you just adjusted. Take out all the basting threads and return the fabric to its original flat form; then bond the muslin to a firm backing. Any of these methods will result in a very permanent, highly usable pants sloper.

If you are tracing the lines from the muslin to tagboard, be sure to copy each line and all written information onto the permanent pattern. Label each section with the date, your weight and personal measurements. The body *does* change and weight *does* vary; slopers should be upgraded periodically and dating will tell you when your sloper needs some scrutiny (Fig. 134).

Fig. 133. Ease side seams where more room is needed.

When completed, clip the sloper to a hanger and store it in the closet when it is not in use. If you're short of closet space and feel it necessary to store your sloper in some corner, roll it up and put it in a mailing tube. Protect your sloper, keep it upgraded and in good condition, and it will return maximum service for a long time to come.

Using Your Sloper

There are several ways to use your sloper to advantage:

1. Cut pants directly from the sloper.

2. Copy or trace all personal corrections from your sloper to any new commercial pants pattern you buy.

3. Design your own patterns by laying pattern tracing cloth or tissue over your sloper. Trace the prime fitting lines for the personal shape and dimensions while making design changes from the basic style.

The section entitled "Be Your Own Designer" (page 91) has ideas and detailed instructions on using your pants sloper to create comfortable, stylish variations.

Becoming familiar with what constitutes a personal fit and how to achieve this goal makes sewing much easier and far more satisfying. The effort you invest in keeping your measurements up to date and using them to perfect the fit of your slopers (and everything you sew) will pay wonderful dividends: elegant, wearable clothing—a compliment to your craftsmanship.

Fig. 134. With proper fit, one can look elegant even with a protruding stomach.

CREATIVE RESOURCES

There is so much inspiration for fashion designs in our world that you can run out of storage space long before you run out of ideas. Ideas are all around you; they come from everywhere—and they're out there for you to use. Your single sewing resource does not have to be commercial patterns. With your personal sloper you can bring all of your design concepts to life; they can open an entirely new, wonderful world of wearable fashion for you.

Where to Look

Fashion advertising in the daily newspaper has a very real influence on the way you dress. Advertisements keep you apprised of the latest designs, the newest fashion trends, exciting ideas and combinations, and popular color schemes (Fig. 135). Pictures in the newspaper are not drawings of runway clothes from some way-out fashion show. They illustrate what is acceptable and worn in your own local area, available in your local stores.

Newspaper ads include detailed illustrations that show how the clothing is constructed and how a garment can be accessorized. There are examples of finishing details, unusual seam treatments, the use of topstitching, button styles and buttonhole finishes, new concepts for trimmings and imaginative decorations. Fashion illustrations in your daily newspaper graphically demonstrate the current choices for the length of a sleeve or the placement of a hem, the location of a waistline, a new neckline treatment, or a new interpretation for an entire costume (Fig. 136).

Use fashion information personally. Interpret the ideas you see in the newspapers to your advantage; make use of them in your sewing wherever they fit in with your wardrobe plans, thoughts and dreams.

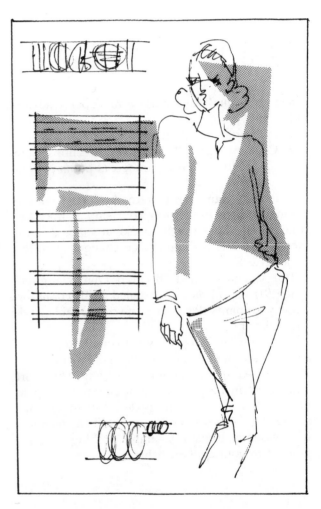

Fig. 135. Borrow ideas from newspaper ads.

Ideas for new fashion designs don't have to come strictly from women's fashion photos and illustrations; details from the latest in children's clothing might inspire a new adult outfit that can't be found ready-made. Your creativity can be sparked by something as small as an unusual zipper placement or other finishing detail or something as extensive as a little girl's dress or jacket. As long as there are ideas out there for you to use, use them.

Men's wear, from fabric through complete garments, has a strong influence on female clothing. Advertising from men's shops offers an abundance of information on the latest trends in tailored dressing, tips on both fad and fashion. You can see graphic examples of long or short jackets, pleated or plain-front pants, patterned or simple shirts.

Not sure about the placement of pockets for the latest garment on your sewing machine? Men's wear is where the cargo pockets began, plus lots more that women have made everyday items in their wardrobes.

A men's wear advertisement might even induce you to wear something you haven't put on since you were a child: suspenders. You'll find wonderful things in men's wear ads.

Fashion magazines come out every month with literally hundreds of clothing ideas. The photographs and drawings on each page are another source of inspirational material for your sewing. Each drawing and photograph is accompanied by information on the fabric, color scheme and accessories to put the whole look into effect. The information includes tips on hairstyles and make-

Fig. 136. Use all ideas freely.

up to complement the clothing, the mood of the new trends, types of clothing that can be combined, visuals of what works and what doesn't. You'll find regular monthly articles on what's new in fashion: shapes, style, and fit, along with details on what the top designers are planning.

Fashion writers in all these magazines keep the public informed (in great detail) about the current trends that exert influence not only on the coming season but for the next year or more. Photographs and illustrations on the pages of fashion magazines include garments you might not get to see anywhere else, bring you up to date on the clothing shapes for now and the coming season, and explain the mood of the new fashions. They supply answers to your fashion questions: heel heights for various skirt lengths, when and how to wear gloves and/or hats, which fabrics are most popular this season and what decorative details will be fashionable for seasonal wear.

Women's Wear Daily is an excellent fashion publication; it is the newspaper of the fashion industry. Because it comes out so often, you might find some friends who would like to share a subscription with you; there are more than enough issues in a single subscription to go around several times. Even an occasional copy purchased at a local newsstand is a treasure trove of inside information on the latest fashion trends—enough to carry you through several seasons of sewing and inspire a closetful of clothing.

Sewing magazines, both monthly and bimonthly, have drawings of the latest pattern releases from commercial pattern companies as well as methods for cutting garments without using patterns. They give a lot of information on fabrics and how to add special touches to a design. They supply updated information on techniques, such things as making shoulder pads, new methods and unusual notions to make all your sewing easier.

There are a lot of new fashion magazines directed towards specific groups: the slender young figures, the very sophisticated, the trendy, the athletic types, or the ample women. Lately, designers, becoming aware of the special needs of the handicapped, have been coming up with special fashions; these are being picked up by many publications. The drawings, photographs and detailed, written descriptions are all out there, all waiting to inspire your creativity.

Free Information

If you feel that you're buying too many fashion magazines each season, take a trip to the public library. You will find a complete selection of books, magazines and even videos that demonstrate the simple and intricate of sewing skills and fashions— new patterns and examples of how the finished garments look in motion. Most of these treasures are available for you to take home by showing your current library card; others are classified as reference material and are limited to library use only. But they *are* there for your use, at no cost. That could free some additional money for your sewing budget.

Television has become a source of fashion information. Excerpts from international fashions hows are run as regular weekly features, and time is being given to national broadcasts of sewing lessons and information. Check your local TV scheduling to find out when these are available in your area.

Organize for Your Designs

When something in a library book or magazine catches your fancy, make photocopies or sketches of that style or design. Please don't cut anything from library publications; others want to use them, too. Clip illustrations or photographs from your own publications to include with the photocopies from library books. Organize your reference material—clippings, photos and other related information—into a personal fashion notebook to prevent the loss of any miscellany.

Get into the habit of translating your ideas and creative inspirations into detailed sketches. Include your own drawings and notes with the other information collected in your notebook; you'll soon build a portfolio that will be invaluable to your future sewing.

YOUR FASHION NOTEBOOK

The purchase of a ring-binder, a set of dividers, pockets and unlined paper is a good way to start organizing clippings and fashion notes (Fig. 137).

Fig. 137. Start a fashion notebook.

• Plastic pockets are available at stationery shops, all punched and ready to fit into a binder. They are perfect for storing clippings and transparent so that you won't have to overhandle the information.

• A large package of unlined notebook paper is suitable for sketching designs with pencil or pen.

• Dividers will separate your notes and ideas according to types of clothing: blouses, dresses, skirts, pants and accessories, etc. Label the dividers for easy access to your information. You'll have everything at your fingertips without groping.

Preserve fabric samples by taping bits of exciting, interesting or unusual fabric onto the pages of your notebook. When you come up with a design suitable to a particular fabric, move the fabric sample to the page that holds that drawing. You won't be tempted to buy as much random yardage until you know what you're going to do with it. When you do buy, your purchases will have adequate yardage for the designs, and you'll be better prepared for what you plan to sew.

Make notes and sketches in your folio on commercial pattern segments that can be incorporated into future garments. The armhole treatment you liked on a blouse might work well for a new dress, the sleeve from an old dress pattern might just spice up that blouse pattern you weren't too sure about. List the name of the pattern company (if it is from a commercial pattern) and the number of that pattern, and detail how you plan to use it in an extended design.

If you have an idea of combining segments from several patterns, list each segment, identify the pattern number and company, and sketch your concept of the finished garment (Fig. 138). Seeing something drawn on a sheet of paper helps firm up the design and point you towards the best possible fabrics and finishing details. File the drawing in your notebook until you're ready to purchase fabric and notions; then take your drawing with you as a shopping guide.

Fig. 138. Sketch your fashion ideas.

When you sew a design from your notebook, detail the information for that garment on the page with your illustration. List the date, the amount of yardage used, the notions required, and anything else that might help you the next time you use the pattern. Tape a scrap of the fabric used for the actual garment to the page and note your thoughts about the garment. Maybe while you sewed you had ideas for a different type of collar or sleeve, methods to simplify construction, or changes in the finishing treatment. You'll be amazed at how helpful your own hints will be to your future sewing, and how important and inspiring your notebook will be to your clothing designs and wardrobe planning.

BE YOUR OWN DESIGNER

The three perfect-fitting slopers you've created are the stepping-stones towards that ideal wardrobe you've always wanted. They are the tools that guarantee the fit of every garment you craft (Fig. 139). You can finally dispose of those garments in your closet that are not to your liking—garments that just don't feel or look right. The dream of having a wardrobe fit to perfection is within your reach.

Familiarize yourself with your basic slopers before you try to create new patterns. Experience the fit of the finished garments you cut directly from your slopers. It will give you a better feel for extending the designs.

When you start designing your own clothes, make good use of the sketches that were previously discussed. Translating your thoughts into a drawing is very important. A design carried in your imagination is elusive. Thumbnail sketches complete with notes on the color and fabric to complement these future patterns will still be available next week, next month or next year, long after a mental concept is forgotten.

When a design is worked to the point where it is ready to turn into a wearable outfit, take out your slopers. Decide how you will translate the drawing into an actual garment.

Use newsprint or tissue to draft pattern segments. Trace the prime lines from each of the slopers involved in the design. Draw the flat shapes for the paper pattern that can be worked into a finished garment. Remove the excess paper from the pattern, pin it together and try it on. Pleat and fold, pin or tape, forming the pattern pieces to the shape of your design ideas. This will give you a view of how well your ideas are developing. Vary the lines by adding or subtracting style-ease until you arrive at a workable pattern.

Experiment with a new neckline or try some styles you've never worn before. Change the length of the pattern segments: skirt, bodice and/or sleeves. Each of the things you do will inspire further thoughts on personal design articulation (Fig. 140).

Fig. 139. Design the clothes you want to wear.

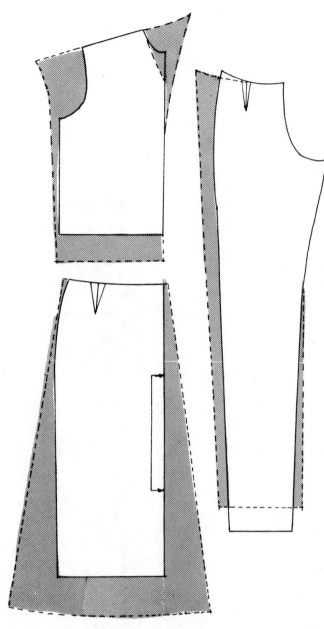

Fig. 140. Design from your slopers.

Combine slopers for one-piece costumes. Experience a jumpsuit with the correct fit or design a new cocktail dress or a gown for the big social event. In other words, put your imagination to work and bask in the results.

If you can't handle your designs from paper, buy some fabric to create a "muslin"—any sort of inexpensive fabric will do. Be sure to use a solid, not a patterned fabric; plaids or prints influence the basic design.

Cut, drape and machine-baste the muslin. Try on your creation to see how the design is working, how the pattern fits and whether changes are necessary. Use either the cloth or paper pattern to cut your creation from wearable fabric. The test fabric can be reused at a later time for other experiments.

Keep enough inexpensive material on hand to be able to create freely (Fig. 141). Many fabric shops offer a discount for quantity buying; a small bolt of fabric could be economical enough to warrant the investment. It is wise to have "throwaway" fabric available for those moments when you want to design a new garment or try out a new concept. Many an inspiration is lost in the time it takes to put away your equipment and run out to a fabric shop.

When you've completed your design and worked it into a pattern that is ready to cut, take it with you to the local fabric shop. You can get a lot of help from the people who work there. The shopkeeper or a salesperson can check your pattern and help you determine how much fabric you'll need for your design. They might offer suggestions to improve the pattern, simplify construction of the garment or extend the design. They can also offer a lot of information on fabric choices, proper buttons for your garment or the latest sundries to improve the quality of your sewing. A fabric shop is a wonderland to the home sewer as well as a place of inspiration for future sewing projects.

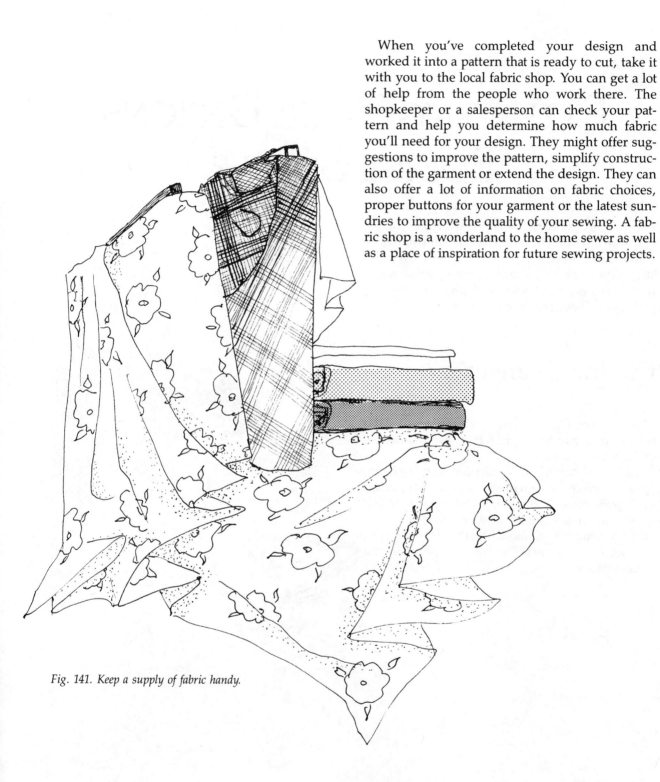

Fig. 141. Keep a supply of fabric handy.

EXTENDING YOUR DESIGNS: BODICE SLOPER

Use your sloper as it was drafted before you attempt any design changes. Craft one or two classic shirts with different finishing details. Then try a shirt with some simple cutting changes that won't require an additional pattern. Work into designing with your sloper one step at a time.

Cutting Changes

Many pattern changes can be effected during the cutting of a garment rather than by drafting an entirely new pattern.

Instead of cutting the shirt front in two pieces, cut a one-piece front on the fold of the fabric, creating a pullover style (Fig. 142). This top can be finished with an assortment of different necklines to vary the pattern even more. Plan the shape, depth and finish of the neckline before laying out the pattern pieces.

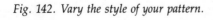

Fig. 142. Vary the style of your pattern.

Necklines for One-Piece Front

A neckline that was designed for a button-front shirt is not large enough to pull over your head without some adjustment.

1. Modify one shoulder seam to accept a zipper, buttons or snaps, which will solve the problem of access (Fig. 143). Extend the neckline facing to include a facing for part of the shoulder seam at one side, both front and back. Sew a zipper in the shoulder seam line between the outside fabric and the facing, for a very different look. Pipe or band the neckline.

Try small buttons and buttonloops for a more elegant closure (Fig. 144). Interface the opening.

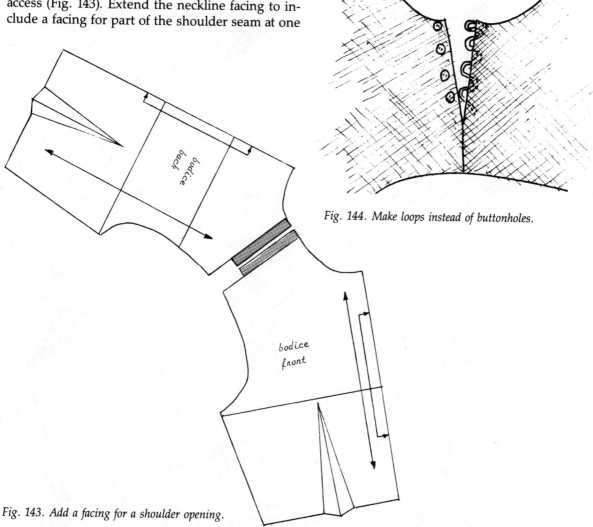

Fig. 144. Make loops instead of buttonholes.

Fig. 143. Add a facing for a shoulder opening.

2. Cut a V at the center of a one-piece front, dropping the lowest point of the V approximately 4 inches below the collarbone (Fig. 145). The depth of the opening can easily be adjusted up or down for comfortable entry and personal modesty. Trim the neckline with matching or contrasting bias piping for a firm finish that neither buckles nor bags.

3. Create a boat neckline (Fig. 146). Widen the neck opening to 6 inches. Drop the front and back of the neckline an additional inch and curve the opening into an oval.

Cut a facing for the new neckline, plan a bias strip of fabric, or sew lace seam binding around the entire opening for a neat finish. Fold the binding to the inside and topstitch in place.

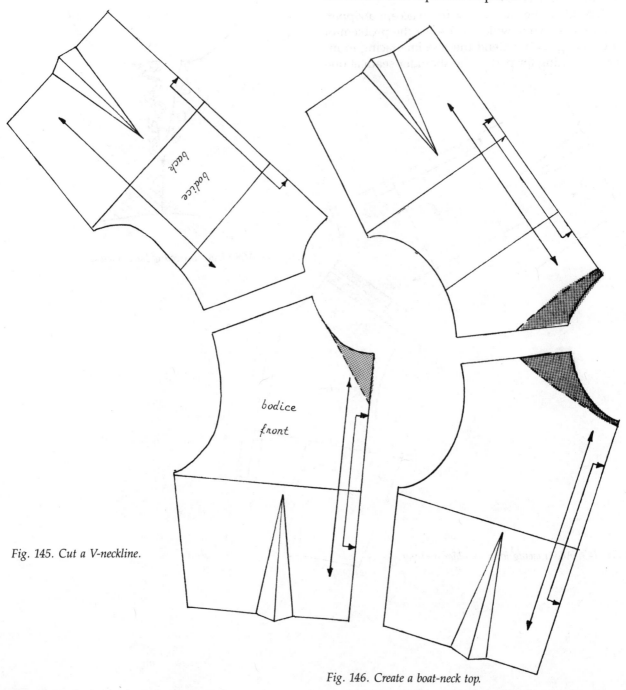

Fig. 145. Cut a V-neckline.

Fig. 146. Create a boat-neck top.

4. Cut the back of the neckline as it is on the pattern but deepen and round the front into a U-shape, approximately 3½ inches below the center front (Fig. 147). Face the neckline.

5. Cut 1 inch deeper (or deep enough to admit your head comfortably) around the entire neckline (Fig. 148). Ease ribbing around the opening for a handsome sweatshirt look. Add ribbing to the bottom of each sleeve and around the bottom of the shirt to complete the look.

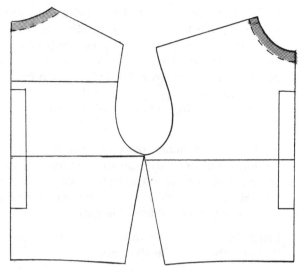

Fig. 148. Cut the neckline deeper to add ribbing.

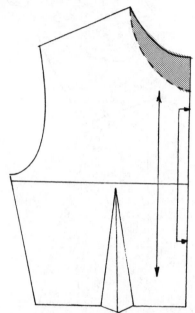

Fig. 147. Round the front for a U-neckline.

Additional Body Styles

HIDDEN PLACKET

A hidden placket requires an additional band and facing to hold the buttons and buttonholes. This band is secured or hidden underneath the blouse front. With a hidden placket, no buttons or buttonholes appear on the outer surface of the garment. This finishing treatment is adaptable to blouses, jackets, coats, skirts, or any type of garment that requires a closure (Fig. 149).

Fig. 149. Use a hidden placket on a variety of garments.

- Cut an additional strip of fabric twice the width of the original facing, fold it in half lengthwise and interface. Sew evenly spaced buttonholes down the center of the strip before attaching it to the front of the garment. The strip is sewn under the facing of the top segment of the garment. A row of topstitching can be sewn along the edge if desired.

Horizontal stitching between every 2 buttonholes will keep the tab from pulling open. Stitch across the tab, catching the facing, not the top fabric of the blouse; the stitching remains invisible on the outside of the garment.

Match button spacing to the buttonholes; sew them on the opposite shirt front.

The Surplice

A surplice bodice is a feminine style that is complimentary to most figures (Fig. 150). It lends itself to a separate blouse or a complete dress. A surplice style can wrap to the back as handsomely as it does at the front. Draft a new bodice front for this style.

Make a few sketches to determine the total appearance of your surplice: how you want it to wrap; how you want it to secure; and where you want the closure to be located.

FRONT-WRAP SURPLICE

There is a wide assortment of choices for the height of the front-bias panel. It can blend into the armhole across the upper chest, fasten below the bosom at the side seam, or meet the waistline at the side (Fig. 151). The closure location is a matter of personal comfort.

The next consideration is the method of securing your surplice-front garment. The two segments of the bodice can cross over at the front and secure at each side with hooks and eyes, snaps, buttons and buttonholes, ties, or any combination thereof.

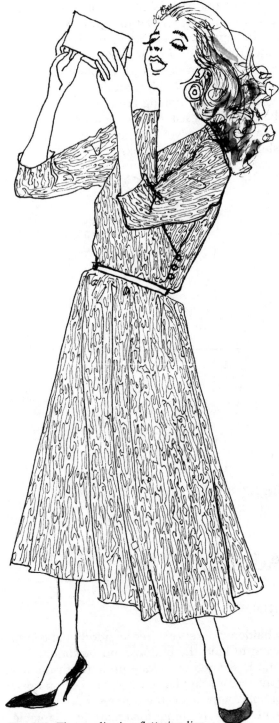

Fig. 150. The surplice is a flattering line.

Changes made to a pattern for a surplice-front bodice do not affect the back of the pattern or the sleeves. Those segments are cut from the original sloper sections. All adjustments are made exclusively to the front-pattern segment. Since the changes are extensive, it is wise to draft a new pattern segment for the front.

• Prepare a sheet of pattern tracing cloth that is wide enough to contain the full width of the bodice front, long enough to include the length from shoulder to hemline plus 3 inches.

Fig. 151. Variations for the surplice front.

This basic surplice wraps from the right and buttons at the left side, at the pattern line indicating the apex of the bosom (Fig. 152). Additional variations for the pattern are detailed at the end of the instructions for drafting the pattern.

• Start by tracing the right shoulder line and approximately one-third of the neckline.

Draw the armhole and complete the side seamline of the right side. Indicate the bustline dart(s) if they are part of the original pattern.

Complete the hemline across the entire front, meeting the opposite or left side seam.

Trace the left side seam from the hemline to the apex where the diagonal line of the front begins.

The final step in drafting the pattern is to complete the neckline at the front. The bias line of the surplice begins at the marked point where the shoulder and neckline meet, moves across and down from the right top at the join of the shoulder and neckline, to the point along the left side seam (under the armscye) where the bodice front fastens.

• Draw the bias line of the front opening with a straightedge to keep it as smooth as possible.

• Draft a facing for the neckline and note that it needs interfacing to keep its shape and fit.

The segment you have just completed is the overflap for the surplice bodice. It will have 3 or 4 buttonholes along the short lefthand edge to secure the bodice on the outside.

• Mark the short extension for evenly spaced buttonholes, starting at the natural waistline for the bottom one, ending ½ inch below the seam line at the top. Whatever the height of the end flap, be sure that there are enough buttons to keep the end from gapping.

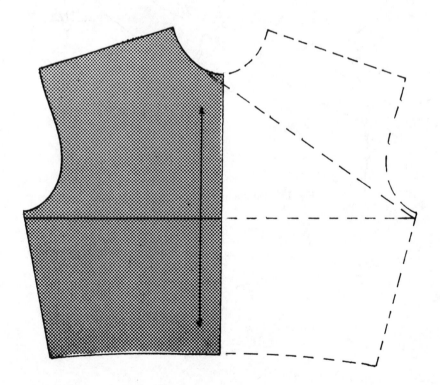

Fig. 152. Draft a surplice pattern.

Cut two fronts for the surplice blouse; be sure you have a right and a left.

The underneath flap is secured inside the blouse to the right side seam with hook and eye or a snap. Use the top button location for the placement of your inside snap or hook.

Double-check all pattern lines, markings and notes to be sure that you have copied, drawn and marked everything correctly.

Keep these additional pattern pieces with your sloper. Once you have drafted a pattern for a design change, it is as reusable as your original sloper.

The surplice style of bodice is adaptable to a sleeveless top, short sleeves, or long sleeves in either dolman or raglan style. It is comfortable for everything from sportswear to elegant evening clothes, from silks to cotton interlock.

Make a surplice bodice with an attached sash (Fig. 153). Add long extensions to the bias fronts that wrap completely around the body and tie, but-

ton or buckle at the back, front or side. Plan the extension as a separate pattern piece, an additional variation for your pattern that can either be taped to the pattern front before cutting or cut later as a separate piece (Fig. 154).

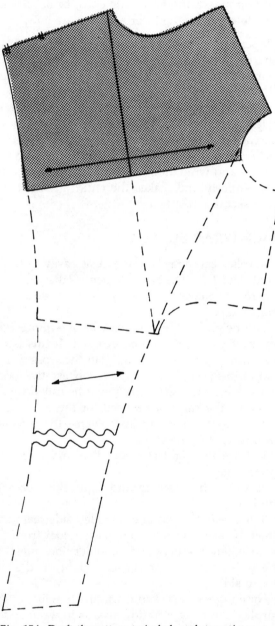

Fig. 154. Draft the pattern to include sash-type ties.

Fig. 153. A sash-wrapped surplice.

• Measure the height of the short left side seam. This is the height of the end that is sewn to the bodice.

The length of the wrap is approximately 70 inches. This measurement is adjusted to the size of your rib cage and waistline measurements. When measuring for the tie ends, be sure to include enough length for an adequate bow.

Taper the band to approximately 3 inches at the narrow end. Mark the wide end: *"Sew to Bias Front."* Mark the opposite or short end: *"Tie End."*

When you sew the right side seam of this wrap-style blouse, leave an opening of approximately 1½ to 2 inches at the waistline. This slit allows the tie-end from the underside to come through to the outside and wrap around the body. It anchors the bodice nicely and makes the entire garment feel quite secure when tied.

BACK-WRAP SURPLICE

A surplice can wrap to the back as easily as to the front (Fig. 155). The back segment of the pattern is where you make changes similar to those for the front wrap.

The height of the surplice will determine how much of your back will be exposed. If this is designed for summer tanning, plan the crossover to end at the waistline. For more conservative occasions, a little less exposure might be called for.

Follow the same steps used for the drafting of the front-wrap pattern; just reverse them to the back pattern segment.

1. Trace the right shoulder line and mark the inner edge.

2. Draw the armhole and right side seam to the hem.

3. Indicate the waistline at the left side seam and draw the bias line across the pattern *back* from the point where the neck and shoulder lines meet, to the waistline (or your chosen height) at the opposite side.

For a more exposed sunback, the bias line of the surplice can be curved downwards to wrap lower.

4. Complete the left side seam from waistline to hem.

5. Mark your pattern segment: *"Surplice Back, Cut Two."*

Fig. 155. The surplice wrapped to the back.

MULTI-WRAP VARIATION

A surplice can wrap at both front and back, creating a simple, versatile two-part blouse. As each half is a finished segment, the style can lead to some interesting combinations when several blouses are created from the same pattern, using different fabrics. Multiple garment halves of contrasting fabrics also can be made that work together to form an entire wardrobe from separate pieces. A solid-color two-part blouse with a selection of print halves clothes you in wearable and packable blouses for home or away. By combining different colors and fabrics you can sew an entire wardrobe of blouses in almost no time.

Yoked Smock

Adapt your basic bodice sloper to the best-fitting smock you've ever worn (Fig. 156). You'll enjoy it as a blouse or jacket, over pants or skirt. If you find some elegant fabric, the pattern adapts to an evening jacket, coat or top for skirt or pants. Knee length or to the floor, this style can also be worn as a robe.

The style of smock illustrated has a separate yoke and additional lower body width; enough changes make it worthwhile to create a new pattern from your bodice sloper.

Before you begin, decide on the placement for the yoke seam and choose a finished length for the completed garment. The yoke seam can cut across the center of the armhole (approximately 6 inches down from the shoulder line) or run across the body of the smock at the armscye (approximately 12 inches below the shoulder). A hemmed length of 29 inches works pretty well, but you might want to try some measurements of your own to determine what lengths will work best for you.

Fig. 156. Make a smock from your bodice sloper.

SMOCK FRONT

Yoke

1. Trace the upper portion of the bodice front from your sloper: the shoulder line, neckline and armhole from the shoulder to the length you chose for the yoke (Fig. 157). Add ½ inch for seam allowance. Draw the line for the yoke completely across the bodice pattern.

Label the segment "*Smock, Yoke Front.*" Don't forget to add the date for later identification.

Body

2. On a separate sheet of pattern paper, start the body of the smock from the bottom edge of the yoke (Fig. 158). Add the seam allowance at the top of the lower section of the pattern, or you will find that the finished smock will be too short. Trace the side-seam line and indicate your chosen length.

Draw the upper edge for the body of the smock to the center line of the pattern. Add 2 to 6 inches to the width beyond the center of the pattern piece for gathering.

Complete the line of the center-front edge to the bottom including 1½ to 2 inches for the hem allowance.

SMOCK BACK

1. From the back-pattern segment, draw the back section of the yoke, matching the front for length.

2. Complete the lower portion of the smock back. Add 2 to 4 inches to the width of the lower back portion for gathering. Keep the back consistent with the front in length and width.

3. Be sure to add a seam allowance to each outside line of the new pattern.

4. The sleeves are cut directly from the sloper without any changes. Alter the finished look of the garment, but not the dimensions of the armhole openings.

Note the location(s) for various pocket styles and write the measurement(s) directly on the pattern segment.

To simplify the sewing of this garment, work with complete units. If you're not already using some simple system, try the following construction method. It should shorten your sewing time considerably.

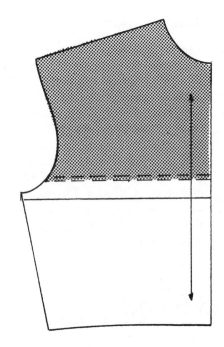

Fig. 157. Draft the yoke first.

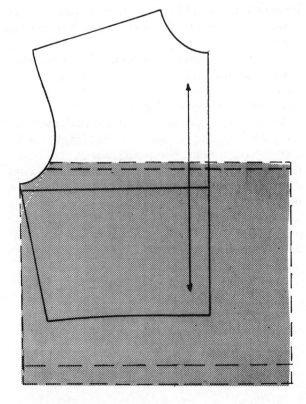

Fig. 158. Extend the lower portion of the pattern.

1. Inseam or patch pockets can be attached to the unsewn segments of the garment.

2. Gather the top edges of both fronts and attach them to the yoke sections.

3. Interface the left and right front facings. Attach to front edges of smock.

4. Sew on the buttons and complete the buttonholes.

5. Gather the lower portion of the back and attach to the yoke.

6. Sew the shoulder seams and attach the collar.

7. Set the sleeves and attach cuff bands.

8. Complete the side seams and sleeves in one continuous line of stitching from hemline, through the armscye and down the length of the sleeve to the cuff.

9. Complete the hem.

10. Enjoy wearing your smock.

Oversize

Although the style is big and comfortable, whatever you've tried on just felt sloppy, not fashionable. Sound familiar? Try cutting oversize garments from your own slopers.

- If you like tops that are "big and comfortable" but you don't like the shoulder seams hanging down around your elbows, cut the shirt ½ inch bigger all the way around the pattern except for the shoulder line.

- Cut the shoulder long enough to drop just over the peak of your shoulder.

- Deepen the armscye by ½ inch to set the sleeve properly.

- Cut the sleeve slightly larger than the size of the pattern.

Raglan Sleeve

Your bodice pattern with slim, set-in sleeves and conventional shoulder line can be adjusted to a raglan sleeve by moving a few lines. Draft an additional pattern to assure the fit of the finished garment (Fig. 159).

Fig. 159. Cut a raglan sleeve in a short length.

Important Note: What is taken away from a segment of the pattern must be added somewhere else. When fabric is removed from the top of the bodice it is added to the sleeve.

Look through your sketches before you begin. Decide on the total design of the new blouse, the finished look for your pattern. How deep do you want the new armhole to be? Where will you locate the shoulder seam? Do you want the original length or a longer one? Is the front to be one piece or with a closure?

Depending upon your height and build, the armscye can be anywhere between the apex of the bosom and slightly above the natural waistline. The finished length of the blouse will have a bearing on the depth of the sleeve. These are personal accommodations from which you will have to choose.

Lay the pattern out on your cutting board as shown in the illustration (Fig. 160). Part of the shoulder line of a bodice is included in the top or extension of the sleeve so the shoulder seams of the front and back pattern segments should be aligned. The edges of the armhole are even; the neckline will be graded to meet.

Fold the top of the sleeve cup under and match the bicep line of the pattern segment to the armscye of the body. The center line of the sleeve points to the join of the shoulder lines of the front and back pattern pieces. Cover the sloper with pattern-tracing cloth or tissue.

FRONT

Trace the neckline and center-front line to chosen length, hem and side seam from hem to apex.

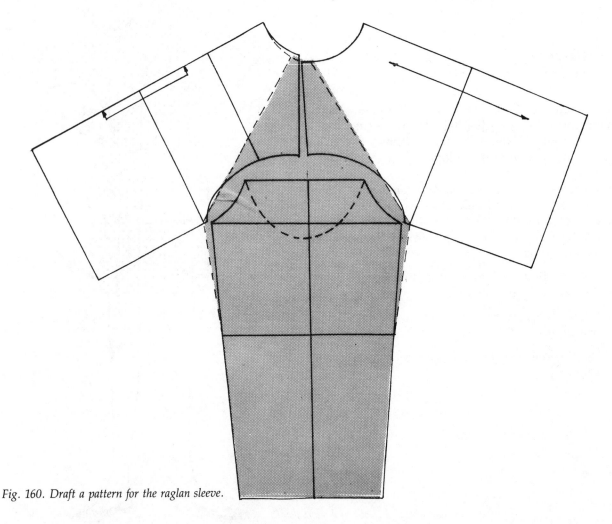

Fig. 160. Draft a pattern for the raglan sleeve.

BACK

Grade the neckline of the back pattern segment to meet the front and trace the new line of the neck. Draw the center back line to match the length of the front portion of the pattern. Complete the side seam to the apex.

SLEEVE

Draw a line from the sleeve elbow to the apex of the body portion, each side. The extra width and depth eliminates the need for a gusset at the armscye. Mark equidistant points on the neckline, both front and back, approximately 1 inch or more from the point where the pattern segments meet. The width of the sleeve top is arbitrary. Choose whatever width you want as long as the spacing between front and back is even. Connect the line from the apex to the marked points at the neckline.

Drafting a New Pattern with Kimono Sleeves

The basic pattern is altered greatly to accommodate this new style (Fig. 161). The new style has sleeve and bodice in one piece, which requires an additional pattern. The body is a loose, easy fit.

Secure the pattern segments to a cutting board as you did to draft the raglan sleeve pattern (Fig. 162). Determine the length for your new top and cover the pattern pieces with pattern cloth or tissue.

Fig. 161. Kimono sleeves of different lengths.

FRONT

Trace the center-front line and extend it to your chosen length. Draw the hemline across the pattern segment.

Widen the sleeve by drawing a line between the elbow of the sleeve and the apex of the bodice. Include the gusset by curving the underarm of the sleeve into the side seam of the bodice. Complete the side seam.

Trace the sleeve and continue the center line to meet the neckline.

BACK

Grade the back neckline to meet the curve at the front. Trace the remainder of the neckline, center back (to meet the chosen hem length) and indicate the hemline.

Connect the elbow line to the apex and curve the line of the sleeve to meet the body. Complete the side seam to the hem.

Separate the front and back segments of the pattern along the center line of the sleeve and add a seam allowance at all edges.

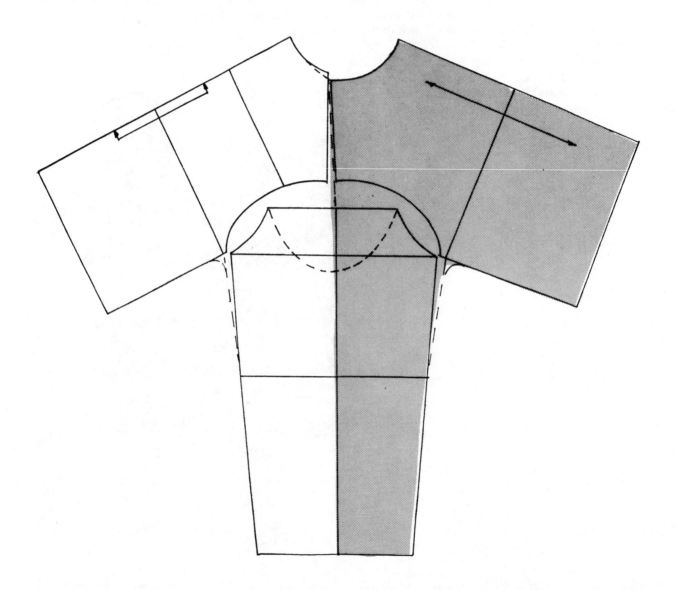

Fig. 162. Draft a pattern for kimono sleeves.

Drop Shoulder with Separate Sleeve

Since the early '40's a dropped shoulder line has been an important fashion statement (Fig. 163). If you have ever had a yen for a dropped-shoulder pattern that truly fitted you, draft it from your personal sloper.

The shoulder line is already indicated when you lay out the sloper segments as you did for the kimono and raglan patterns (Fig. 164).

FRONT

Trace the center front and neckline. Draw the hemline at the chosen length.

The armscye is widened and dropped by extending the line from the elbow to the apex and drawing the gusset curve between the sleeve and body. If you prefer a loungier style of shirt, widen the bodice to the extent of the addition by redrawing the side seam to the width of the armscye.

Fig. 163. Dropped shoulder line.

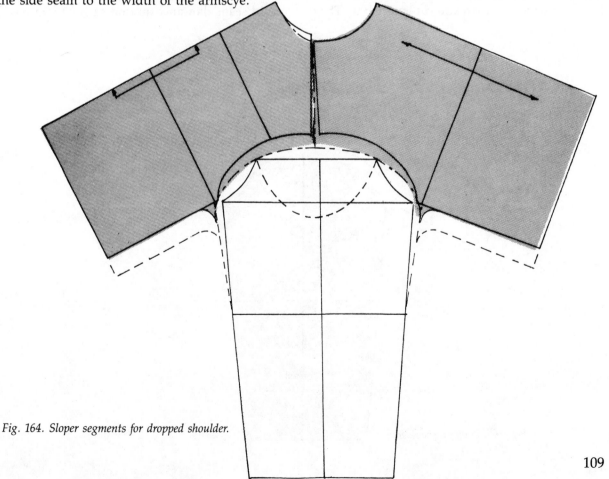

Fig. 164. Sloper segments for dropped shoulder.

Sleeves

The important thing to remember when revising a pattern is that the shape of the finished garment is always based on your personal measurements. Variations result from adding style-ease to your basic sloper dimensions. This means that your sloper sleeve pattern is easily adapted to an assortment of lengths and widths without requiring new pattern segments. Anything from a cap sleeve to bracelet length is already marked directly on your pattern.

To use any pattern segment that you've marked with a variety of lengths, crease the pattern along the chosen line and fold under that portion of the pattern not needed for the style you plan to cut. Do not cut your sloper for any reason other than future size adjustments.

Become familiar with the pattern augmentations that result in full sleeves, balloon sleeves, bell sleeves, or butterfly sleeves. Most of these alterations can be made when you cut your fabric. They are variations that don't really require separate patterns.

SHOULDER LINE

Draw a new shoulder line for the bodice. Indicate the top seam between the front and back segments and continue the line halfway to the sleeve top. Flatten the curve of the armhole by connecting the shoulder and armscye across the fold of the sleeve cap.

BACK

Grade back neckline to meet the front. Trace the center-back line and draw the hem at the same length chosen for the front.

Complete the armhole as you did the front.

SLEEVE

Follow the curve created by the armhole to complete the sleeve top (Fig. 165). Sketch the seam lines and hem including the facing at the bottom.

Add seam allowance around each pattern piece.

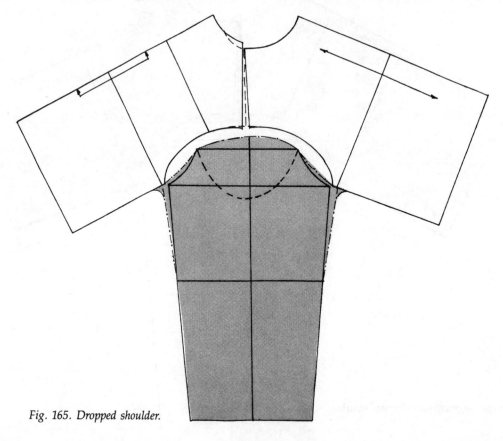

Fig. 165. Dropped shoulder.

110

CUFFS

Vary the finishing on the sleeves of your shirts. Your style can be as simple or ornate as you choose, but it does make the difference between ho-hum and a personal statement.

- Try elastic at the end of the sleeve. Add enough length to the sleeve to include a casing or band the lower edge instead of making a full cuff.

- A barrel cuff or French cuff is always elegant.

- Put gauntlet cuffs and fancy rhinestone buttons on your next dressy shirt.

Make free use of your imagination when you feel that you have "nothing to wear." Your slopers are always ready to reinterpret into tomorrow's styles. They are the matrix for designing new clothing with confidence.

Variations for the Skirt Sloper

The basic skirt sloper will yield any number of variations. Just don't lose the fit of the original pattern in creating new styles.

Fig. 166. Close a wrap skirt to the front or the back.

Wrap Skirt

A front- or back-wrap skirt can be cut from the sloper with just a few simple adjustments (Fig. 166). There is no need to draft a separate pattern for the design.

FRONT WRAP

The front is comprised of two panels, each containing ¾ of the total front segment of the pattern (Fig. 167). This provides a generous overlap for the front of the skirt.

- Lay the pattern on the unfolded fabric. Draw around the segments with tailor's chalk or a sliver of soap to achieve full pattern pieces before you cut.

  Draw the front segment to the center line: side-seam line, waist and hem. Fold the front of the pattern down the length through the dart. Turn it over to the opposite side (for the right half of the front). Place the folded pattern on the fabric next to the first segment. Match center, hip and hemlines. Trace around the second half of the skirt front.

  Cut two panels from the front segment, a left and a right.

- Cut a 3-inch-wide facing for each front. These should be interfaced for stability.

- Cut a single back section on the fold of the fabric as indicated on the sloper.

- Choose the type of closure you want and cut the waistband. (A wrap-and-tie waistband requires more fabric length than a button waistband.)

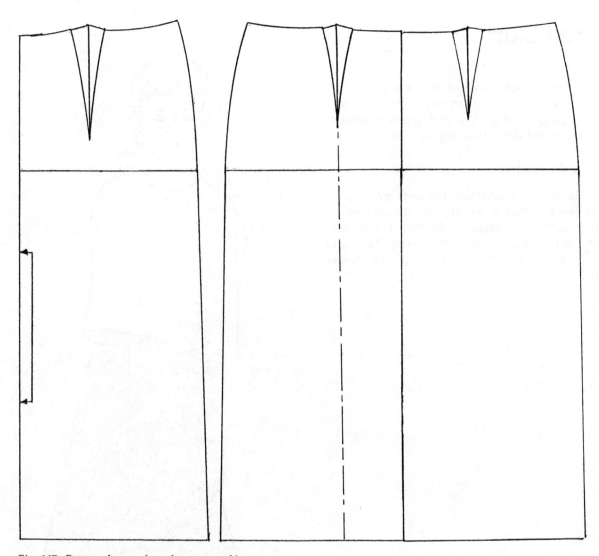

Fig. 167. Pattern changes for a front-wrap skirt.

BACK WRAP

Make the skirt as a back wrap by reversing the cutting order: Fold the back segment of the pattern down the length, through the dart, and cut two back panels. Cut one front on the fold of the fabric.

Complete the skirt as you do for the front wrap.

Gored Skirt

Translate the simple, straight-line skirt sloper into a gored skirt. The design can be planned for either six or eight gores (Fig. 168). Each panel is fitted to the hipline and flares from hip to hem.

SIX-GORE SKIRT

Keep the design consistent: The number of gores in the front should be repeated for the back of the pattern. The new pattern is drafted in four segments: center front, side front, center back and side back. Start from the front of the sloper (Fig. 169).

Fig. 168. A gored skirt is very graceful.

114

Front

1. Cover the sloper with pattern-drafting cloth (paper). Trace the hip and hemlines of your skirt completely across the page.

Center Panel

2. Approximately 1 inch in from the right edge of the page mark the waistline and draw the perpendicular line of the center front, to the hem. (The center front is cut on the fold.)

3. Draw a second vertical line parallel to the center front, from the bottom of the dart to the hem. This is the seam line of the center panel.

4. Trace the sew line for the dart to the waist. This provides the hipline shaping without the bulk of additional fabric and stitching.

Flare

The center-front panel flares 1½ inches, on each side. The flare of each panel widens towards the back to give the skirt a flattering sweep. Where panels meet in a common seam, the lines take a matching flare; the opposite seam line widens.

5. Mark a point 1½ inches outside the seam line, along the hem. Connect the point to the line of the hip at the seam line. Curve the hemline slightly (within the gore) to prevent the hem from hanging in points.

6. Label the segment: *Center Front, Cut One on Fold of Fabric.*

Slide the pattern paper far enough to clear space for the remaining front section. Align the pattern paper with the markings for the hip and hemlines.

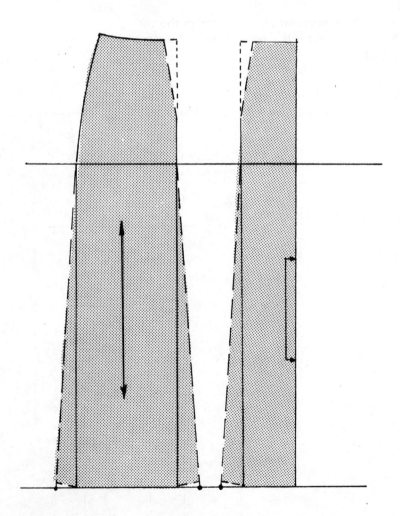

Fig. 169. Pattern adjustments for the front of a six-gore skirt.

Side-Front Panel

7. Trace the waist, hipline curve and side seam to the hem.

8. Draw a straight line from the bottom of the dart to the hemline.

9. Complete the sew line of the dart to the waist.

Flare

10. Mark a point 1½ inches outside this line and connect it to the outside point of the hipline.

11. The side seam line is where the flare starts to widen slightly. Mark a point 2 inches outside the side seam (at the hemline) and connect it to the outside point of the hipline.

12. Curve the hemline slightly within the width of the gore.

13. *Label the segment:* Side Front, Cut Two.

Back

Secure the back segment of the sloper to the cutting board and cover with a second sheet of pattern paper (Fig. 170).

Trace the hip and hemlines completely across the page.

Center Panel

14. Approximately 1 inch from the edge of the paper, mark the center-back waist and draw a perpendicular line to the hem.

15. Draw a parallel line (seam line of the center-back panel) from the bottom of the back dart to the hem.

16. Complete the dart sew line to the waist.

Flare

18. Mark a point 2½ inches outside the seam line, along the hem, and connect it to the outside point of the hipline.

19. Curve the hem within the 2½-inch gore.

20. Label the segment: *Center Back, Cut One on Fold.*

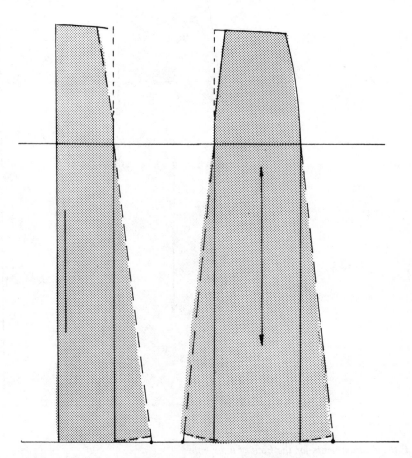

Fig. 170. Pattern back adjustments for a six-gore skirt.

Side Back

Slide the pattern paper to clear the center segment. Align the back-side panel at the hip and hemlines.

21. Trace the waist and hipline curve. Complete the side seam to the hem.

22. Draft a parallel line from the bottom of the dart to the hem. (This seam joins to the center-back panel.) Complete the line to the waist along the sew line of the dart.

Flare

23. Where this panel joins the center-back panel the flare is 2½ inches. Mark the hem (on the drop line from the dart) and connect the point to the hipline.

On the opposite side, where the panel joins the side seam of the front, the flare is 2 inches. Mark the hemline and connect to the hipline with a diagonal line.

24. Curve the line of the hem within the gores.

25. Add the seam allowance around all segments and be sure to mark the bottom of each panel for the hem facings.

The preceding information (for drafting a gored

Fig. 173.   Fig. 174.

skirt) can be applied to any number of design changes.

- Match a tunic top to a short, very flared six-gore skirt (Fig. 171).

- Do a tulip- or trumpet-style skirt by starting the flare halfway between the hip and hemlines, or add godets for a little extra flirtiness (Fig. 172).

- Flare an 8- or 10-gore skirt from the waistline for a generous A-line (Fig. 173).

- Widen the flare generously along the hemline for a flirty dance skirt (Fig. 174).

GODET

A godet is a triangular insert that can be used between straight panels of your skirt to create a similar appearance to that of the trumpet skirt (see Fig. 172). It provides an added dimension as godets can be cut from matching or contrasting fabric for a color or texture change. They can even be cut as squares or diamonds to vary the hemline.

Fig. 171.   Fig. 172.

Cut the skirt from six or more panels. The godets can start from mid-thigh or 2 to 3 inches above the kneecap, depending upon the length of the skirt and the amount of flounce desired.

Tiered Skirt

A straight, tiered skirt will team well with a short or long jacket. It is a practical style for anyone's wardrobe because it is tailored enough to go to the office or a meeting, dressy enough to pair with a cocktail top for evening. And it can have a secret life: a third tier that can make the skirt ankle or floor length for very dressy occasions (Fig. 175).

The length for each segment of the skirt is determined by the length you prefer for your finished skirt. The pattern illustrated measures 32 inches.

To be effective, the second tier should be at least 12 inches long, hanging a minimum of 10 inches below the upper skirt.

First Tier (overskirt): Fold the pattern to your chosen length. The pattern illustrated is 21 inches from the waistline, including a 1-inch hem.

Cut the overskirt from your sloper, flaring the side seams slightly along the lower 3 inches of the side seams (Fig. 176).

Second Tier (underskirt): This portion lines the first tier across the hips and hangs below the hem first-tier-tunic-style (Fig. 177). The underskirt is a two-part construction.

1. Cut the entire upper portion from the original sloper using lining material to eliminate added bulk from the finished skirt. The length shown is 19 inches including seam allowance.

Fig. 175. Variation for a tiered skirt.

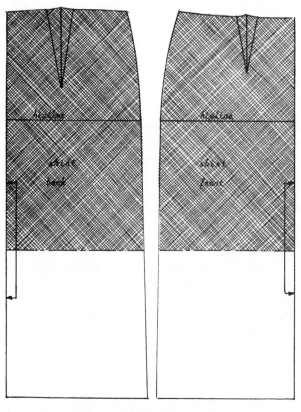

Fig. 176. Cut the tiers directly from your sloper.

2. The remainder of the underskirt is cut from the skirt fabric. The cut length of this portion is 14 inches, including a top seam allowance and a bottom hem facing.

CONSTRUCTION

Sew the side seams.

Complete the hems for each tier separately.

Stitch the two "skirts" together at the waistline and put in the zipper.

Attach the waistband.

A long evening look is achieved for this skirt by making a third tier, a separate skirt with a slip-like top.

1. Cut the upper portion of the separate underskirt from tricot. Use your sloper for shaping but don't sew the darts. A slip-top doesn't require shaping—just enough width to pull on over the hips.

Fig. 177. Pattern for second tier of skirt.

2. The cut length of the tricot portion is 1½ inches shorter than the total length of your sloper.

3. Substitute elastic at the waist for the usual band.

4. A skirt-fabric band is sewn to the bottom of the tricot slip. The length of the finished skirt-fabric segment is from 2 inches above the hem of the skirt to the floor (or to your ankle, if that is your evening length preference).

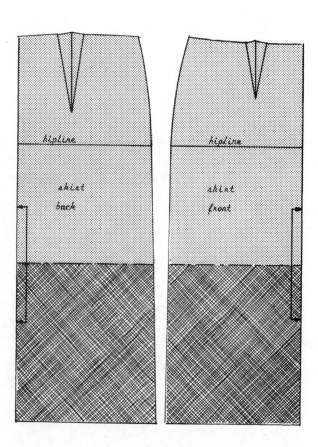

Yoked Skirt

Alter your sloper to include a yoked top; it's a nice change of pace. Any number of lower segments can be attached to the well-fitting yoke (Fig. 178).

The sloper can be folded at a flattering length for cutting a yoke. If you prefer a pattern for each redesign, draft a separate pattern from your sloper.

The line of the hip across the pattern is a good length to start, but don't make hasty decisions. Stand in front of a full-length mirror, fold the sloper to a variety of lengths and judge for yourself.

If your choice is to draft a separate pattern piece, then prepare two sheets of pattern paper in an adequate size for the front and back segments of your pattern.

FRONT

1. Trace the waistline from your sloper.

2. Measure down to the lowest point you feel will be personally flattering. The finished yoke pattern is marked for folding to assorted lengths for cutting.

Note: Inches removed from one part of the pattern must be added somewhere else to maintain the size and shape of the original fit. When redesigning a pattern to include a yoke, what is removed from the length of the upper segment must be included in the lower segment along with seam allowances for each portion.

BACK

1. Trace the back of the sloper. Mark lengths to correspond with the front.

2. Add seam allowance and hem facings.

There are any number of skirt styles that can be used with a yoke.

Fig. 178. Three variations of the yoked skirt.

Straight Wrap

Create the look of a wrap skirt below the yoke.

Follow the general directions for the wrap skirt (page 112) eliminating the length of the yoke from the top of the wrap segment.

CONSTRUCTION

Sew the back of the skirt to the yoke.

Overlap the two front sections, pin in position and stitch to the yoke.

Sew side seams from hem to waist.

Attach the zipper and complete the side seams, waistband and hem.

Flounce

There are several approaches to a gathered lower portion for a yoked skirt. One is to cut the lower skirt segment as a circle skirt, starting from the hipline instead of the waist (see Fig. 178 on page 120).

The formula for finding the radius of the top line of the circle is: (hip measurement divided by 3) + length to bottom of yoke = radius of upper line of circle.

The formula for the hem of the circle portion is: (hip measurement divided by 3) + personal skirt length = radius of hem.

1. Take the total measurement of your hipline, all the way around, and divide the number by 3.

2. Add the length of the yoke to the radius of the circle. This is the measurement to position the upper line on the pattern. It drops the circular portion of the skirt to the hip.

3. The lower line or hemline is measured from the yoke or hipline to the true hem: R + (hip to hem) = hemline circle.

Example: If your hipline measures 45 inches, divide by 3, which equals 15 inches. Add 9 inches (the length of the yoke) to 15 inches (⅓ of hip measurement). The tape measure is extended to 24 inches for the upper line of the skirt.

Assuming that your chosen skirt length is 35 inches, subtract 9 inches (the length of the yoke is already added to the first measurement). This brings you to 26 inches (the length from the yoke to the true hem). Add the measurement for the radius of the top circle and you have 50 inches for the hemline radius (the point at which you draw the hemline).

A skirt this length (35 inches) requires 50-inch fabric for the lower portion.

Open the fabric and iron out the center fold. Refold the material matching the selvages. The size of the folded piece must be large enough to include the total radius of the circle (length from fulcrum to hem: 50 inches).

Lay the fabric on the cutting board or on the floor; wherever you can spread the fabric to its full extent, and keep it flat and unwrinkled.

- Stick a hat pin into the end of a tape measure and pin it securely to the folded corner of the fabric.

- Extend the tape 24 inches (substitute your hipline radius) and use a sliver of soap or tailor's chalk to mark the line as you move the tape around to the other edge of the fabric.

- Extend the tape to the full length of the fabric, 50 inches (substitute your hemline radius), and mark the circle for the hem.

Cut along the marked lines.

Sew darts and complete the yoke, inserting a zipper at the side seam.

Sew the seam of the lower portion of the skirt, forming a circle. Pin the circle to the lower edge of the yoke, easing in any excess fabric, and sew. Try not to pull the circle where the fabric is on the bias as this will change the hang of the fabric.

Let the skirt hang out for a day or two without finishing the hem; the circle portion might sag unevenly. After the garment has relaxed, try it on. Check the hemline and cut away any uneven areas. Complete your hem.

Asymmetric Hemline

Cut the yoked circle skirt with an asymmetric hemline (see Fig. 178). Mark the top circle on the fabric. Move the tape measure several inches off the center point of the circle (along the selvage) before drawing the hemline. Use the same length to define the hem. The lower circle will have a decided dip on one side.

Additional Yoked Skirts

Anything you can dream up by way of a skirt style can be applied to a skirt with a yoke.

- Make a series of bias-cut strips, wide enough to meet the length to the hem. These are stitched together and gathered into the hem of the yoke. This results in a perky skirt that can be completed with several tiers of ruffles at the bottom instead of just one (Fig. 179).

- Permanent pleated fabric can be sewn to the yoke (Fig. 180).

- Shorten the yoke until it just covers your hip-bones. Cut a straight style, inserting pockets along the yoke seam (Fig. 181).

- Fashion an asymmetric yoke to top a skirt (Fig. 182). Slits or inverted pleats finish the hemline. Topstitch for added interest.

Use your favorite source of inspiration to create additional styles. Skirts sew up quickly, extending your wardrobe and multiplying the use of jackets and tops—another way to make an important and personal fashion statement.

Fig. 179.   Fig. 180.   Fig. 181.   Fig. 182.

DESIGN WITH THE PANTS SLOPER

Familiarize yourself with the fit and feel of your personal sloper before you attempt to create new designs (Fig. 183). Using quality fabric, cut a pair of pants directly from the master pattern. Plan and execute the finishing details to enhance the basic pattern; *then* try some of the variations that are detailed on the following pages. Every idea listed won't necessarily be your cup of tea but read all the information; ideas can trigger new thoughts to suit your needs and desires.

The next step is to work out some designs of your own. Study your sloper and decide which variations can be handled from the basic pattern as you cut the garment and which variations will require a separate pattern.

Chart the details for your pants sloper that can put new life into your casual wardrobe. Add pockets or pleats, roll the cuffs or stitch them into a traditional form, gather or pleat the waistline, add a drawstring, widen the legs or narrow them to leg-skimming slimness (Fig. 184). Everything is easy when you know how to go about it.

Sloper Variations

FRONT PLEATS

A good place to start extending your pants sloper is with the addition of pleats on either side of the zipper. Pleats are usually added exclusively to the front portion of the pattern (Fig. 185) unless you want very full, baggy-type pants, in which case pleats can be added all around.

Fig. 183. Use the sloper before you try variations.

Decide how many pleats you would like to have and how deep you want them. One pleat on each side of the center-front seam can be folded from the fabric allowed for the darts indicated on the pattern front. This revision is done with no pattern changes. Anything beyond one pleat will need some additional fabric which can be allowed for along the outside seam edges.

Fig. 184. Design variety into a single pattern.

Fig. 185. On the most pants, pleats are only in the front.

One Pleat

• Stitch the back darts in the conventional manner. Fold a pleat from the front-dart allowance (Fig. 186). Pin the pleat at the waistline and stitch into the waistband as you complete the garment.

Press the pleat lightly for approximately 2 to 3 inches to hold the shape. This creates the illusion of a pleat with no changes to the pattern.

Multiple Pleats

If you opt for two or three pleats and your pattern has only one front dart, add to the width of the front portion of the pattern only (Fig. 187).

1. Measure the depth of a single pleat and double the amount to include the return. Note the total measurement for the single pleat on your sloper.

2. Decide how many front pleats you will add and multiply the measurement of the pleat by the number of pleats you plan to add to one side.

3. Add the result of your measurement to the width of the pants along the outside seam line. Grade the new seam line to flow into the existing cutting line between the widest point of the hip and the waist.

4. Fold and press each pleat. Stitch the pleats into the waistband.

5. For a crisper finish topstitch each pleat along the folded edge for 1 inch to 1½ inches. The stitching will help them lie better and keep a sharper crease.

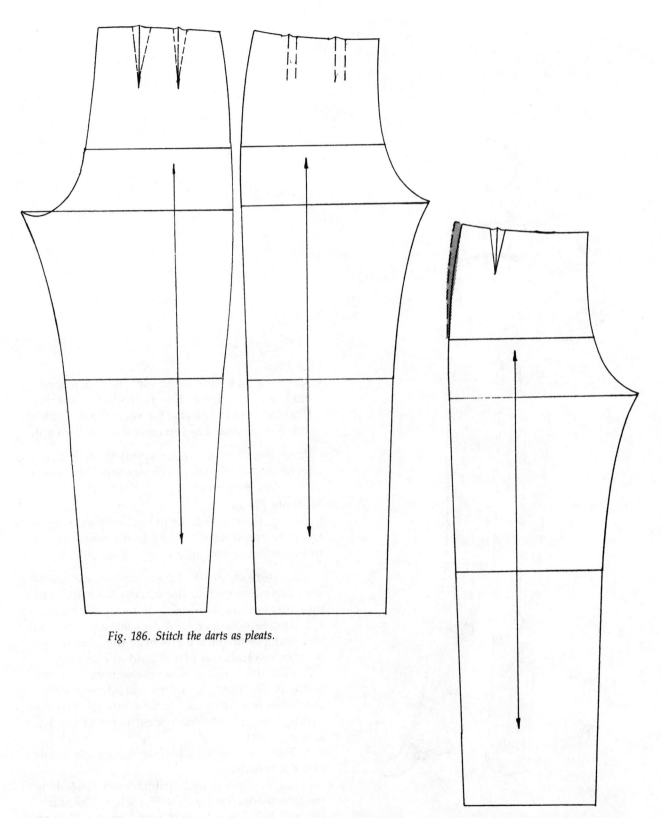

Fig. 186. Stitch the darts as pleats.

Fig. 187. Widen the top of the pattern for additional pleats.

ALL-AROUND GATHERED
OR PLEATED TOP

For looser pants (baggies) that are gathered or pleated completely around the top, both front and back, cut straight up from the widest part of the hipline to the top or waistline of the garment on both the front and back pattern segments (Fig. 188).

• Reshape the cutting line along the top edge to accommodate the curve of the waistline and include the extra fabric. Allow the center of the pattern to dip down at the front to accommodate the curve of the natural waistline and rise at the back for seat room.

• The center front 2 inches (either side of the zipper) is stitched into the waistband without any gathering. The remainder of the fabric is gathered or pleated evenly, front and back, to fit the waistband.

Use caution when you pin the top of the pants to the waistband; loosely fitting pants can be deceptive. Keep the side seams and the fabric grain lines straight. Don't pull the side seams too high into the waistband or you will create wrinkles across the tops of the thighs.

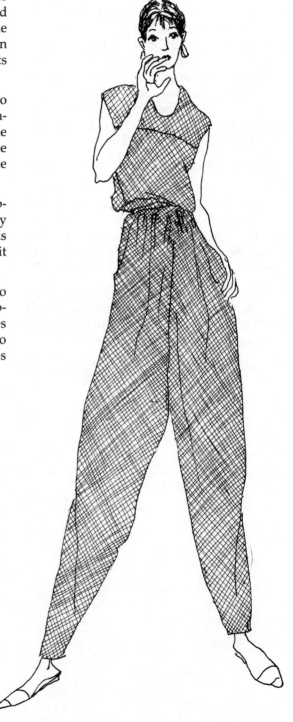

Fig. 188. Sew baggies from your straight-line sloper.

127

Pull-on Pants

Pull-on pants are usually made from *knitted* or *stretch* fabric. They rely on the built-in give of the yardage and an elastic waistband for their fit (Fig. 189). Pants of stretch or knit fabrics need no additional wearing-ease, just your body measurements. What they do need is a little extra room at the top to slide comfortably on and off over the hips, the widest part of the body. Pull-ons are cut almost straight up from the widest point of the hip to the waist (Fig. 190).

- Eliminate the darts (the contour of your body shapes a knitted garment).

- Redraw the outside seam line from the widest point of the hip to the waist. Mark a point ½ inch outside the waistline at the top and taper the seam into the original line at the widest point of the hip.

- Add a 2½-inch-wide casing (long enough to go around the top of the pants) and elastic (1-inch elastic, 2 inches less than your actual waistline measurement) to complete the pants.

Fig. 189. Your body shapes pull-on pants.

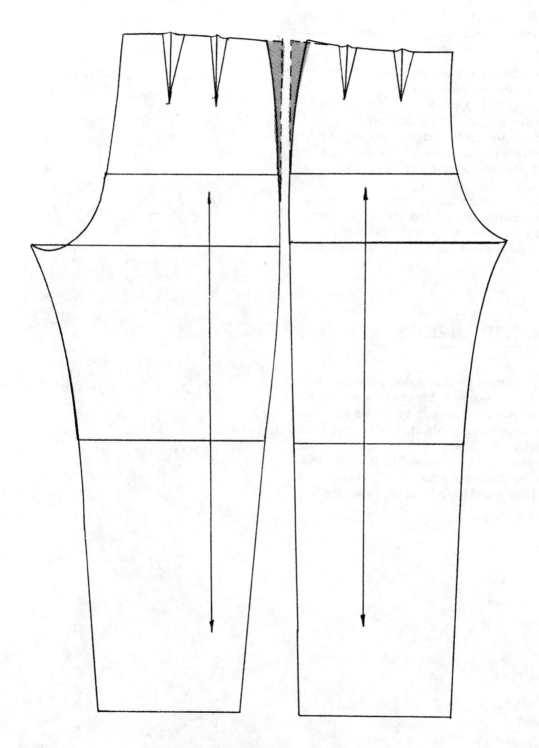

Fig. 190. Cut pull-ons straight up from the hipline.

Sewing Details

This is a fast-sew method for pants. If you have never tried this method, give it a try—it might save you a lot of time.

1. Sew the two fronts and two back sections together along the crotch/rise line.

2. Sew the outside seams joining front and back.

3. Sew the inseam in one continuous line of stitching from the bottom edge of one leg, up to the crotch (where you reinforce the stitching by going back and forth a couple of times) and down the other leg to the bottom edge.

4. Attach the waistband and elastic. Try on the trousers to assure the fit and check the hems. Make any final adjustments at this point.

5. Complete the hems and enjoy your new pull-on pants.

Drawstring Pants

Adjusting a pattern for drawstring pants (without a zipper) is very similar to the changes made for a gathered or pull-on pant with an elastic waistline (Fig. 191). Drawstring pants are usually cut from *woven* fabrics with little give. They rely on wear-ease and shaping for access and fit (see Fig. 190). The addition of the drawstring provides the room along the waistband to slide on over the hips.

Fig. 191. Drawstring pants are cut the same as gathered or pull-on pants.

Fig. 192. Vary the width of the pant legs.

You can restyle for the design as you cut the pants; you do not need to draft an additional pattern.

1. Cut the outside seam line straight up from the widest point of the hip to the waistline with no shaping. This extra width at the top of the pants will allow the waistband to clear the hips easily without tearing the fabric or straining the seams when you don the finished garment.

2. The rest of the pattern is cut without any changes.

3. The waistband strip is cut to the same measurement as the top of the pants, the widest point of the hipline.

4. Insert eyelets at the center front of the waistband before attaching to the garment. Eyelets allow the drawstring to pull freely without excessive wear to the fabric. This waistband needs no interfacing.

5. Cut the drawstring long enough to go around the waist plus enough length to tie at the front. Insert 4 to 6 inches of elastic at the center of the drawstring to allow it to breathe with you.

6. Include whatever style of pockets you prefer.

7. Sew the pants together by the method detailed above or by a method of your own choosing.

Pant-Leg Widths

The width of pant legs is easily adjusted to follow the latest style trends by simply changing the angle of the seam line (Fig. 192). This alteration can be made when cutting the garment. If you would rather have a separate pattern for leg-style changes, draft new patterns from your sloper.

Measure the width at the bottom of one pant leg, add or subtract the appropriate amount on either side of the leg, both front and back, and grade the new seam line to blend into the existing one (Fig. 193).

Keep your fabric in mind when adjusting the width of the pant legs. Crepe, sheer woollens, flowing silk or jersey will obviously look more luxurious with a wide sweep of fabric, but they will also lie smoothly, even cling a little, when cut slim.

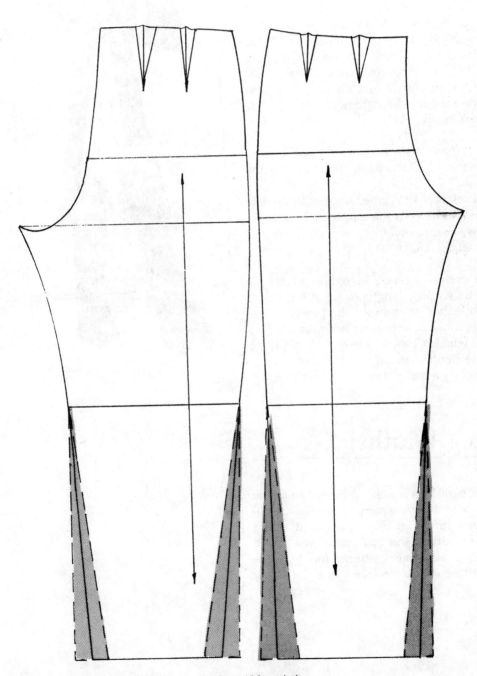

Fig. 193. Pattern changes for leg-width variations.

Heavy taffeta or brocade, corduroy, rough tweeds, etc., don't have the soft flow of the lighter weight yardage and will stand stiffly away from the body. These fabrics could add bulk to your figure when used for wide-leg pants.

STRAIGHT LEGS

When the out-seam line falls straight from the widest point of the hip to the hem, and straight along the inseam, the pants are said to have moderately wide legs (Fig. 194). In years gone by, these trousers were called slacks, Harlow pants or Oxford Bags. To create this look with your pants sloper:

Fig. 194. Wide leg pants.

- Drop a metal tape or yardstick straight down along the outside seam line of the trouser leg from the widest point of the hip to the hem and redraw the line of the leg (Fig. 195). Remove any shaping from the pant leg as you redraw the outside seam and cutting lines.

- The inseam should be checked to see that it, too, falls straight from knee to hem without any tapering, both lines parallel. This creates a nice swing to the pant legs when you walk or dance.

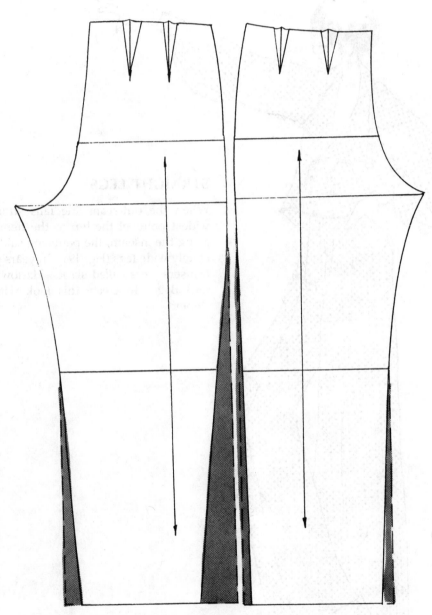

Fig. 195. Pattern adjustments for pant-leg variations.

ULTRA-WIDE LEGS

For extremely wide-legged pants, the angle of the seam lines will be out or away from the leg. This includes all extra-wide pant legs such as palazzos or pajama-culottes (Fig. 196). They are created in much the same manner as the wide-leg pant detailed in the above paragraph except that the angle of the seam line spreads as it moves towards the hem.

- Place one end of your straightedge at the widest point of the hipline and move the opposite end of the yardstick out, away from the hem of the pant leg. The width along the hemline is optional; make these pants as wide as you'd like.

- Drop the inseam line straight down from the point where the crotch and inseam meet to the hem with no shaping. When you remove the shaping from the inseam, the pants fall in a smooth, skirt-like flow.

Palazzo-style pants look best when the hemline barely grazes the floor. They have the look of an evening skirt and the comfort of pants.

Fig. 196. Ultra-wide pant legs.

SLIM-LEG PANTS

For tapered legs, both seams (inseam and outside line) angle in towards the leg (Fig. 197). This is how stirrup pants, capris, or very fitted jeans are created.

- If your pant sloper was designed to fit closely in the thigh area, taper the leg only from the knee to the hem.

- Measure your foot around the instep and heel to be sure you have enough width at the bottom of the leg for easy access. Narrowing pant legs beyond the point where your feet have easy entry requires zippers or other closures at the bottom of each leg to allow you to slip them on and off.

- Narrow each leg to the width you desire.

Cropped Pants

You don't have to do any pattern alterations to cut cropped pants. When you marked the sloper with alternate lengths, you did all the measuring necessary. The cutting line you use should already be labelled "Cropped Pants" or "Ankle Length." Make the cropped style pants by folding your personal pattern along the shorter hemline and cut the fabric at that point (Fig. 198).

Fig. 197. Slim-leg pants.

136

Culottes

To make skirt-like culottes, the pattern changes are to the legs only (Fig. 199). You can either make a separate pattern for culottes or make your adjustments while you cut. Again, as with cropped pants, your chosen length is premarked and labelled on the pattern. Cut along the premeasured guidelines for the length; widen the lines of the legs as you cut the width.

• The outside seams are cut straight down from the widest point of the hipline to the hem.

• Follow the slight curve at the top of the inseam for the first inch; then cut straight down to the hem. The little curve at the top of the inseam prevents the fabric from bunching and riding up as you walk. Do not taper either leg seam.

Shorts

Choose a length for shorts that is flattering to your figure and legs (Fig. 200). Cut the shorts from the hemline length designated on the pattern. The pant leg of the sloper is folded under along this line for cutting. An additional pattern is not necessary.

Fig. 200. Shorts can be flattering.

Fig. 198. Fold the pattern length under to cut cropped pants.

Fig. 199. Culottes cut from the original sloper.

Maternity Pants

Maternity pants can be adapted from your sloper (Fig. 201). A U-shaped opening is cut at the front using the points of the hipbones to mark the width of the opening across the top. The cutting lines are usually synonymous with the center of the darts but you should check your own pattern to be sure those points work for you.

Just above the crotch bed curve is the positioning for the depth of the U at the bottom.

Insert a commercial maternity panel in the front opening or use ribbing, available by the yard, cut to fit the space. This will provide the grow-room needed for the stomach area without distorting the general shape of the pants. Pants are much more flattering when they fit properly; start from your own sloper for the best look.

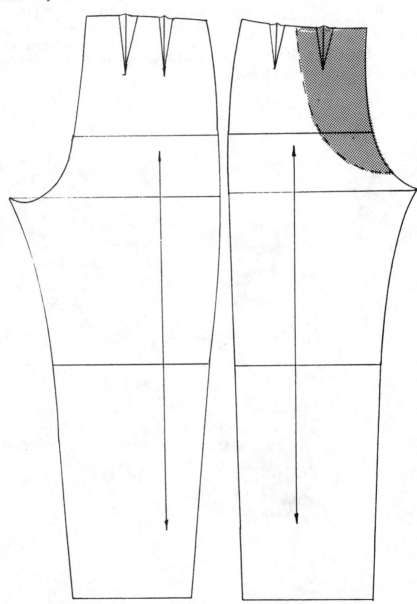

Fig. 201. Make your own pattern for maternity pants.

138

COMBINING SLOPERS

Basic Combinations

Although the basic slopers are designed as independent units that produce a beautiful array of separates, they also merge into an assortment of beautifully fitting wardrobe staples, such as dresses and jumpsuits.

- A combination of the basic shirt and skirt slopers produces a timeless, tailored shirtwaist dress (Fig. 202).

- Add a gored or full-circle skirt to the basic shirt pattern and you further extend the possibilities (Fig. 203).

Fig. 202. Left: A tailored dress from basic slopers.

Fig. 203. Right: Vary a tailored dress by changing the skirt.

- Incorporate some of the suggested bodice changes (see "Extending Your Designs: Bodice Sloper," page 94), and the design potential for your slopers multiplies geometrically (Fig. 204).

Fig. 204. Another variation from your basic pattern.

- Use the shirt with the pants pattern and you have a perfect-fit jumpsuit (Fig. 205).

- Add an open overskirt to your pants or jumpsuit and you're on your way to a wardrobe of elegant at-home clothes (Fig. 206).

Master patterns provide an unusual opportunity for personal dressing; they encourage your options and designs. The choices of style, color, combinations and finishing touches are your own; you create the personal aura.

Fig. 205. Even a jumpsuit can fit perfectly.

General Information

Don't attempt to just sew the basic bodice and skirt patterns together in a hit-or-miss manner and expect them to work as a single unit. The lines of both patterns must be adjusted to flow into each other when combined into a single garment (Fig. 207).

1. Grade side seams and darts of the bodice, skirt and/or pants slopers to flow into a single line from armscye to hemline.

Fig. 206. Add an aura of glamour with an overskirt.

2. Compare existing darts on upper and lower segments. Be sure they meet at the waistline. Realign darts where necessary.

3. To combine the patterns, the hemline for the bodice needs extra length to blouse gracefully at the waistline. Add a seam allowance after altering the pattern. This is important to prevent the bodice from being too short.

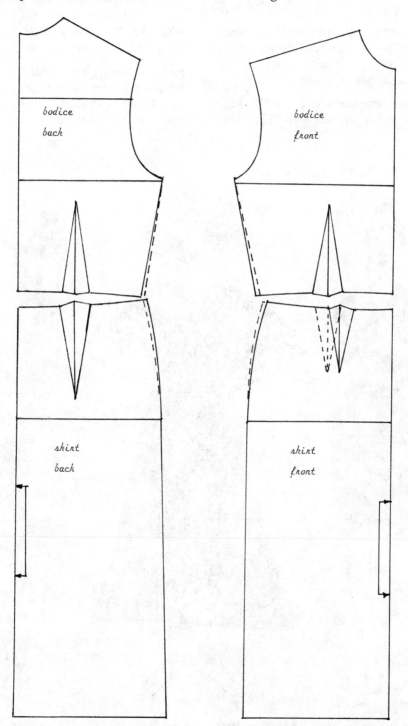

Fig. 207. Adjust patterns to work as a unit.

Variation: Surplice and Skirt

One of the major design revisions for the bodice sloper was the surplice. Incorporate this wonderful style into a dress pattern. It can be sewn in so many versions and fabrics.

- Combine the surplice bodice with a straight skirt, and it is an elegant, all-purpose style (Fig. 208).

- Combine the surplice bodice with an A-line, dirndl or wrap skirt. Each skirt style totally changes the look of the finished dress (Fig. 209).

- Make a surplice dress that wraps both front and back and you have the "Ultimate Dress" (Fig. 210). You have created a half-dress that can be the basis for uncounted changes.

Sew a two-part dress from a single fabric. Make additional segments (or complete dresses) from a coordinated fabric and you have a total wardrobe that can take you everywhere.

Fig. 208. Variation: Surplice bodice with straight skirt.

Fig. 209. Variation: Surplice bodice with full skirt.

Fig. 210. Variation: Two-way wrap dress.

For example: Try black matte crepe for the original dress, a surplice bodice combined with a slim skirt. Use satin or lace for a second dress. The surplice top for the second garment is cut from the same pattern, but this time combine the top with a circle skirt. The result is a striking, interchangeable party-wear assortment (Fig. 211).

Fig. 211. Combine portions of different wrap dresses for unlimited variety.

- Use the surplice-front pattern to design a double-breasted jacket (Fig. 212). Sewn in an unlined, unconstructed manner, the jacket turns a simple sheath into an elegant costume that makes a bold and authoritative fashion statement.

Fig. 212. A surplice bodice pattern becomes a double-breasted jacket.

Bodice and Pants

A comfortable jumpsuit is the product of the basic bodice and pant slopers. There are a lot of options open when you create your own styles.

- Sew the bodice pattern with a dolman sleeve for the top of the jumpsuit (Fig. 213).

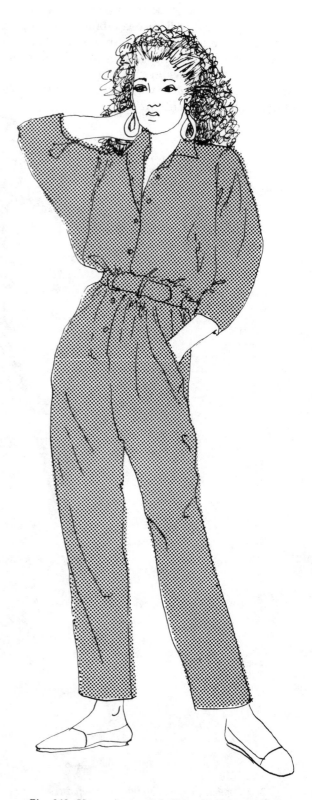

Fig. 213. Vary a jumpsuit bodice with dolman sleeves.

- Combine the top with a 2- or 3-pleat pants style (Fig. 214). A wide, softly crushed belt will set the finished garment off beautifully.

Fig. 214. Add or subtract pleats for more variations.

• Create a surplice top and blend it into a palazzo pant with an asymmetric close (Fig. 215). There is no need for zippers with this style: A snap on the under portion and a button for the top will keep the entire jumpsuit in place.

Fig. 215. Palazzo pants and surplice top eliminate the need for zippers.

- Widen the top and pants patterns to create a trendy, oversized jumpsuit for summer-fun suit or bathing-suit cover up (Fig. 216).

Fig. 216. A trendy jumpsuit.

Planning the Design

1. Work out the design in a thumbnail sketch. Personal style preference will dictate whether the jumpsuit will be fitted and classic, loose and trendy, casual or dressy (Fig. 217).

2. Decide if the jumpsuit is to have a waistline seam or a seam down the center with the top and bottom cut in one piece.

3. Consider an appropriate length for the sleeves and legs. A seasonal jumpsuit should suit the weather: a short-sleeved or sleeveless top with cropped legs for summer wear, long sleeves with full-length pants for winter.

Figs. 217–220. Thumbnail sketches visualize ideas.

Do you want full sleeves or fitted? Cuffed, banded or loose?

4. Choose a flattering neckline finish (Fig. 218). For a collarless style you might consider a round, crew, boat, V, banded, or asymmetric neckline.

Collar styles could include any one of the following: cowl, turtleneck, Peter Pan, Eton, Chinese, funnel, or even a hooded neckline.

5. Locate the opening. Will it be at the front, off-center or centered; or the back, one piece or two?

A conventional, front-opening jumpsuit can have a placket for the buttons and buttonholes, or merely a facing. A zippered front can work with or without a placket.

Consider buttons for the upper portion of the jumpsuit, a zipper below the waist.

Back openings can either have a zipper down the entire length of the body or just a closure to slightly below the waist.

Maybe you'd like a pull-on style with elastic at the neckline for access.

6. The last major decision is the style for the bottom portion of the jumpsuit. Would you get more use from a jumpsuit with full or narrow legs? Regular length, cropped (ankle length) or even shorts? Do you prefer your trouser legs cuffed, straight or rolled?

You want the maximum pleasure from the clothing you design. Everything mentioned above should be taken into consideration before finalizing any decisions. Making sketches of every possibility before you start drafting your pattern is an essential tool in that process.

Figs. 221–224. Draw alternate finishing details.

Drafting the Pattern

When you arrive at a design for your jumpsuit,
find yourself a place to work that is out of the
household traffic pattern. Pick a corner with
enough space to spread out your slopers and pattern paper without everything getting stepped on.
Pin or tape your design in a convenient spot for
easy viewing, lay out pencils, pens and pattern
paper and start drafting that pattern.

Fig. 225. Give yourself plenty of room to work.

• Begin with the bodice. Plan your pattern sections to complement the sketch you drew. Draft the body and sleeves; then put away the bodice sections so that you can clear the space before you begin the pants or lower section of the jumpsuit.

• If you are partial to certain collar styles, create a template for each one that you can use with your basic bodice sloper. This is a simple way to extend the use of your pattern.

• Work out the lower portion of the jumpsuit with your pant sloper. Grade the seams to meet properly at the waistline. See that the darts are matched for upper and lower segments.

• Verify the seam lines and be sure a seam allowance has been added to all portions of the pattern that have been revised or altered.

Here are a few footnotes to this garment, some additional details: For a buttoned, center-front closure, you can use a separate placket. To get an idea of a width that will be complimentary to your figure, measure the finished plackets on several different garments in your closet. Go with the width that you like the best.

Placket and facing can be cut as a single unit. The measurement for the placket is: Double the width (front and facing) plus 1 inch for the seam allowance. This measurement includes a ½-inch seam allowance for each side. If you are used to sewing with ¼-inch seams, reduce the amount of seam allowance.

The length of the placket is a combination of the measurements for the center fronts of the two patterns: from the neckline of the bodice to a point just above the beginning of the crotch curve on the pants. Be sure to add a seam allowance for the top and bottom of the placket when you write the total measurement on the pattern.

When you are ready to sew the placket to the jumpsuit, fold the placket in half lengthwise, interface the entire length and stitch it to the garment.

Take your pattern sections when you shop for the fabric. The pattern sections can be laid out on the fabric for a more accurate measure of the yardage necessary to complete the garment.

You might see some pieces of material that would work up into additional garments for the current or future seasons. When fabric suggests designs for future pattern changes, sketch the ideas directly on a pattern segment. You can copy the drawing into your sewing notebook when you return home.

Once you've gotten this far you probably are very assured about construction methods for any garment. Just in case you ever feel a momentary doubt, the directions from commercial patterns can answer most of your sewing questions. If the answers to your problems cannot be found in the direction sheets, the major pattern companies have a hot line that you can call for help. Telephone Directory Assistance, or your local library can supply you with the proper numbers for your area.

EPILOGUE

Fashion is what YOU make it. . . .

You come to terms with the body in which you live, learn how to enhance your assets and minimize any deficits. As you wander through life you absorb information about fashion: past, present and projected. All the while, you perfect your sewing ability.

You choose a fabric because it catches your eye. It speaks to you in a personal way. It stirs your imagination. It has no real form of its own except for what you perceive, what you sense within that fabric. Until it is formed into the raiment to enhance your body, a bolt of cloth is merely a flat ribbon of color and texture. You are the one who cuts that fabric; you are the one who shapes it with stitching—stitching that brings it into a new dimension. *You* create a fashion.

Slip into the finished garment, allow the molded material to glide over your body, and your body gives it the life *your* imagination responded to when that piece of cloth first caught your eye.

You have made a personal statement, produced a style, crafted a personal expression. You have

Fig. 226. Make a personal statement.

154

turned an inanimate length of cloth into a living, breathing work of art. You have expanded a concept into a unique object: a covering specifically made to enhance *your* body.

On the hanger this creation quietly droops in the darkness of your closet waiting for you to bring it to life, to give it movement and form. Each time you wear it you feel a new sense of pleasure, excitement and accomplishment.

The power to be creative is within each of us. We are all born with imagination—albeit of varying degrees. For some this power is nurtured, for others it is repressed, but it is there to be used, to be exploited, to be expanded.

The time to nurture your imagination is now: Yesterday you weren't ready, tomorrow is for other things.

Broaden the scope of your knowledge to ensure the best possible personal choices. Take pleasure in fashion. Use it to your advantage; don't let it use you. Make a personal statement, and do it with style (Fig. 226).

METRIC EQUIVALENCY CHART

MM—MILLIMETRES   CM—CENTIMETRES

INCHES TO MILLIMETRES AND CENTIMETRES

INCHES	MM	CM	INCHES	CM	INCHES	CM
⅛	3	0.3	9	22.9	30	76.2
¼	6	0.6	10	25.4	31	78.7
⅜	10	1.0	11	27.9	32	81.3
½	13	1.3	12	30.5	33	83.8
⅝	16	1.6	13	33.0	34	86.4
¾	19	1.9	14	35.6	35	88.9
⅞	22	2.2	15	38.1	36	91.4
1	25	2.5	16	40.6	37	94.0
1¼	32	3.2	17	43.2	38	96.5
1½	38	3.8	18	45.7	39	99.1
1¾	44	4.4	19	48.3	40	101.6
2	51	5.1	20	50.8	41	104.1
2½	64	6.4	21	53.3	42	106.7
3	76	7.6	22	55.9	43	109.2
3½	89	8.9	23	58.4	44	111.8
4	102	10.2	24	61.0	45	114.3
4½	114	11.4	25	63.5	46	116.8
5	127	12.7	26	66.0	47	119.4
6	152	15.2	27	68.6	48	121.9
7	178	17.8	28	71.1	49	124.5
8	203	20.3	29	73.7	50	127.0

YARDS TO METRES

YARDS	METRES	YARDS	METRES	YARDS	METRES	YARDS	METRES	YARDS	METRES
⅛	0.11	2⅛	1.94	4⅛	3.77	6⅛	5.60	8⅛	7.43
¼	0.23	2¼	2.06	4¼	3.89	6¼	5.72	8¼	7.54
⅜	0.34	2⅜	2.17	4⅜	4.00	6⅜	5.83	8⅜	7.66
½	0.46	2½	2.29	4½	4.11	6½	5.94	8½	7.77
⅝	0.57	2⅝	2.40	4⅝	4.23	6⅝	6.06	8⅝	7.89
¾	0.69	2¾	2.51	4¾	4.34	6¾	6.17	8¾	8.00
⅞	0.80	2⅞	2.63	4⅞	4.46	6⅞	6.29	8⅞	8.12
1	0.91	3	2.74	5	4.57	7	6.40	9	8.23
1⅛	1.03	3⅛	2.86	5⅛	4.69	7⅛	6.52	9⅛	8.34
1¼	1.14	3¼	2.97	5¼	4.80	7¼	6.63	9¼	8.46
1⅜	1.26	3⅜	3.09	5⅜	4.91	7⅜	6.74	9⅜	8.57
1½	1.37	3½	3.20	5½	5.03	7½	6.86	9½	8.69
1⅝	1.49	3⅝	3.31	5⅝	5.14	7⅝	6.97	9⅝	8.80
1¾	1.60	3¾	3.43	5¾	5.26	7¾	7.09	9¾	8.92
1⅞	1.71	3⅞	3.54	5⅞	5.37	7⅞	7.20	9⅞	9.03
2	1.83	4	3.66	6	5.49	8	7.32	10	9.14

INDEX